The Girl's Guide to Life.

HENDRICKSON
PUBLISHERS

ROSE
KiDZ.

Check out all of the books in
The Girl's Guide Series

The Christian Girl's Guide to Being Your Best

The Christian Girl's Guide to Friendship

The Christian Girl's Guide to the Bible

The Christian Girl's Guide to Your Mom

The Christian Girl's Guide to Change

The Christian Girl's Guide to Money

The Christian Girl's Guide to Style

The Christian Girl's Guide to Me: The Quiz Book

The Girl's Guide to Your Dream Room

The Girl's Guide to LIFE.

The Girl's Guide to Life.

Sherry Kyle

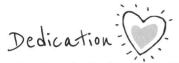

Dedication

For Marcia Smith, and all of life's experiences we've shared together. You're special to me and I love you LOTS!

THE GIRL'S GUIDE TO LIFE.
© 2015 by Sherry Kyle

RoseKidz® is an imprint of
Rose Publishing, LLC
P.O. Box 3473
Peabody, Massachusetts 01961-3473 USA
All rights reserved.

Cover and interior design: Laura Skibinsky

ISBN: 978-1-58411-149-8
RoseKidz® reorder#: L48220
JUVENILE NONFICTION / Religion / Christianity / Christian Life

Printed in The United States of America
Printed October 2018

Table of Contents

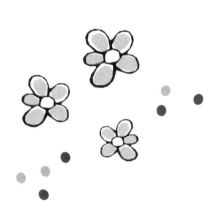

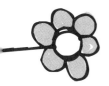

Hey Girlfriend!
Welcome to **The Girl's Guide to Life!**

When I was a girl your age, I wanted to be grown up. I dreamed of the day I'd have my own place, own my own car, and make decisions all by myself. I imagined the man I'd marry and how many kids I'd have. Life would be perfect. But as I grew, I discovered that life can be difficult and making good choices can be hard. Even the little things like annoying siblings, or getting a bad grade on a paper can drive you crazy.

I discovered that God loves us and cares about all our problems. He wants the best for us. In fact, he desires that we have a relationship with him. We can talk to him any time of the day and he'll hear us. With God by our side, we'll never be alone.

Ever wish you had a map to guide you through the maze of life? Well, now you do! *The Girl's Guide to Life* is written for girls just like YOU who want a road map to lead them through life's journey. This book talks about many of the issues girls face today as they grow up to be young adults, such as finding and keeping friends (boys too!), making good grades at school, and standing firm when temptations appear. There are stories about girls your age as well as crafts, activities, quizzes, and tips for extra encouragement. *The Girl's Guide to Life* will point you to the Bible too, the best map of all!

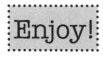

Chapter 1
Life's Not Perfect

Forgetting what is behind and straining toward what is ahead, I press on toward the goal to win the prize for which God has called me heavenward in Christ Jesus.

Philippians 3:13-14

Kaitlyn's Bad Day

Kaitlyn was having a bad day—a very bad day. The outfit she wanted to wear to school was dirty, she couldn't find her homework, and she'd missed her bus. Kaitlyn was sure she got all the problems wrong on her math test, and at lunch she discovered her mom had made her a peanut butter and jelly sandwich *again.* Her best friend, Sydney, decided she wanted to hang out with someone else at recess, and Kaitlyn was the last one picked during P.E. Could this day get any worse?

"Mom!" she called the moment she stepped inside the house. She wanted to hang out and watch TV and forget the last eight hours ever happened.

"I'm right here." Her mom approached with an apple in hand and gave it to Kaitlyn. "How was school?"

"Terrible. Life stinks." Kaitlyn dropped onto the couch. She bit into her apple, the crunching sound loud in her ears. "Can I watch TV?"

Mom's eyes narrowed, then quickly softened. "What happened?"

"I don't want to talk about it."

"Do I need to call your teacher?" Her mother sat beside her.

Kaitlyn shrugged a shoulder.

"What's really bothering you?"

Kaitlyn tucked her hair behind her ear and noticed one of her earrings was missing. Ugh! She'd add it to her "worst-day-of-the-school-year" list. She let out a breath. "It's just been a bad day."

Mom patted her knee. "We all have them every once in a while."

Kaitlyn nodded and sighed. "Yeah, I guess you're right."

"Is there anything specific you'd like to talk about? . . . Because I've got a lot of chores to do before I go to work."

Now that Kaitlyn had said what was on her mind, she wished her mom would talk about it further. But Mom liked the house neat and tidy before leaving for her nursing job at the hospital. Why couldn't she be home all the time like Sydney's mom?

"No, it's okay. Can I watch a show?" Kaitlyn took another bite of her apple.

"Go ahead." Mom straightened the pillows on the couch and picked up the newspaper off the floor.

Twenty minutes into her television program, Kaitlyn caught a whiff of a fishy smell. *Please, no!* "Hey, Mom? What's for dinner tonight?"

"Tuna casserole." Mom called from the kitchen.

Kaitlyn cringed and curled her lip. She slumped lower on the couch. Mom only made tuna casserole when there was nothing else in the refrigerator. She must need to go shopping. Her mind took a turn. Their cat loved tuna casserole. Maybe Kaitlyn could beg her dad to take her and her younger brother out to dinner. A grin curved the corners of her mouth. "When's Dad coming home?"

"Not till late. He's got a meeting tonight. Miss Margaret's coming over soon."

Miss Margaret, an older woman who lived down the street, was the person who stayed with them when her mom couldn't get one of the high school girls to come over. Miss Margaret made sure Kaitlyn did her homework and ate everything on her plate—two things she didn't want to do tonight. Furrowing her brows, Kaitlyn folded her arms across her chest.

What would it be like to have Sydney's life? Not only did her mom stay home, but she took Sydney shopping almost every weekend. Her friend got her nails and hair done at a fancy salon, and her bedroom was huge. Sydney was one of the smartest people in the class, and she could outrun most of the boys. Why did some people have life so easy while others struggled? It didn't seem fair.

Suddenly Kaitlyn remembered a recent conversation she had with her best friend. Sydney complained that her dad was away on business most of the time and that she missed him. It was going to be another two weeks before he'd come home.

Kaitlyn turned off the television, went into the kitchen, and tossed her apple core into the trash. She leaned a hip against the counter. "Need any help?"

"I'm just about done, but thanks for the offer," said Mom. "Oh, by the way, Miss Margaret is bringing her knitting supplies tonight. You've been wanting to learn to knit for a while now . . ."

Kaitlyn didn't know if she could do it. After the day she'd had, she might as well forget the idea right now. "Maybe another time—"

"Come see what I bought today." Mom motioned for Kaitlyn to follow. She opened the closet door and pulled out a shopping bag. "I didn't know if you'd like the purple or the blue, so I bought both." She smiled and took out a bundle of yarn in each color. "I figured once you get the hang of it you might want to make two scarves."

If Kaitlyn learned how to knit, she could make a scarf for herself and one for Sydney—or for her mom for Christmas! Life was looking up. "Thanks."

"I wish I could be the one to teach you, but between my job, keeping up the house, and taking care of your little brother . . ." Mom sighed. "If only I didn't have to work—"

"It's okay," interrupted Kaitlyn. "Nobody's life is perfect."

"You know what? You're right. And God wants us to do our best with the life he's given us."

Kaitlyn hugged the yarn to her chest, a new determination welling inside. "I'm going to forget about my horrible day and learn how to knit."

"After your homework, of course." Mom smiled.

"Oh, yeah." Kaitlyn set the yarn on the kitchen counter and grabbed her backpack.

What do **YOU** Think?

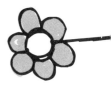

✱ Describe your worst day ever. How about your best day?

_____

_____

_____

✱ Do you ever wish you had a friend's life instead of your own? Why?

_____

_____

_____

✱ How can doing your best with the life God's given you change your attitude?

_____

_____

_____

Tiny Tip It's easy to compare your life with others. Don't fall into that trap. Find something to be grateful for every day. It could be as small as your favorite nail polish or as big as the moon and stars overhead.

Every good and perfect gift is from above, coming down from the Father of the heavenly lights, who does not change like shifting shadows.
James 1:17

Try It! Fabric Prayer Journal

A *prayer journal* is a book that you keep to write down your prayer requests for yourself and others, sermon notes, Bible verses, goals, things God teaches you, and answers to prayer. There is no right or wrong way to keep a prayer journal. You can use a plain spiral notebook or dress it up by making this one.

What you need:

- Notebook or journal
- Fabric
- Lightweight cardboard
- Pen
- Glue
- Glue dots
- Ruler
- Scissors
- Decorations: feathers, glitter, paint, ribbon, stickers, or whatever else you find.

What to do:

1. Open a notebook or journal and lay it on a piece of fabric. Using your ruler, draw a line around that is 2 inches larger than your notebook. Cut the fabric along the line.

2. Once again, lay the opened notebook on the fabric. Cut slits on the fabric where the notebook binding is located.

3. Fold over the edges of the fabric (on the top and the bottom) and glue to the inside of the notebook.

4. Fold over the side edges and glue to the notebook.

5. Cut two pieces of lightweight cardboard 1 inch smaller than the cover of the notebook.

6. Using the same fabric, (or a different one, if you'd like) cut two rectangular pieces that are 1-2 inches larger than your cardboard. Fold over the edges, then glue the fabric onto the cardboard (sides first, then top and bottom).

7. Put glue dots all over the backside of each piece of cardboard and place it on the inside covers of your notebook to give it a finished look.

8. Decorate!

9. Allow to dry.

10. Write in your prayer journal every day. When it's full, read it and discover what you've learned and how God has answered your prayers.

Pray in the Spirit on all occasions with all kinds of prayers and requests. With this in mind, be alert and always keep on praying for all the Lord's people.

Ephesians 6:18

Did **YOU** Know? There is a difference between short-term goals and long-term goals. A short-term goal may be accomplished in a short amount of time, such as finishing your homework or eating your vegetables at dinner, while a long-term goal may take weeks, months, or maybe years to complete. An example of a long-term goal might be saving money or working toward a profession. Setting goals is important and helps you grow as a person.

Teach us to number our days that we may gain a heart of wisdom.

Psalm 90:12

REAL Life 101

LIFE = learning, growing, experiencing the life God created just for **YOU**!

In order to figure out if you're living life to the fullest, consider how you spend your time.

Fill in the blanks:
How many hours per day do you . . .

- Run, jump, move, and play? _____

- Read? _____

- Listen to music? _____

- Watch television? _____

- Play computer/video games? _____

- Do chores? _____

- Spend with your parents? _____

- Hang out with friends? _____

✱Are you surprised at how you use your time?

_____

▭▭▭▷ Out of all the areas listed above, what do you spend the most time doing? _____

_____

✱<u>Learning to use your time wisely is a skill that's developed as you age,</u> but you can begin now to build good habits. One way to have good time management is to hang a calendar on your bedroom wall and fill in each month with all your appointments and activities, such as sports practice, church youth group, doctor visits, family events, and birthdays. (You may need to ask your mom or dad to help you.)

✱<u>Another way to keep you on track</u> is to get a separate binder for school projects and write down your class schedule as well as when projects are due. For example, if you have a book report due in one month, allow the first three weeks to read the book and the last week to write the report.

*Also think about all the things you do in a day

and how long each task takes. For instance, getting ready for bed might take you thirty minutes. For good time management, you'll need to take a shower, brush your teeth, and read your book a half hour before your bedtime. During the day if you are feeling rundown and tired, consider the fact that your schedule may be too full. Are you in more than one sport or too many extracurricular activities? Being too busy can have a negative effect on your health and schoolwork. Everyone needs time to rest. The key to time management is **BALANCE.**

Fun Facts about Life.

* It's impossible to sneeze with your eyes open.

* The average person falls asleep in seven minutes.

* People forget 90% of their dreams.

* Your eyes are always the same size from birth, but your nose and ears never stop growing. YIKES!

* A child's sense of smell is better than adult's.

* It's physically impossible for you to lick your elbow.

* Kids laugh about 400 times a day, while adults laugh on average only 15 times a day.

* No words in the English language rhymes with month, orange, silver or purple.

* There are more chickens than people in the world.

What Does the **Bible** Say?

Each day is a gift from God. **You** can make a difference when you use your time wisely. Look up these Bible verses and fill in the blanks. *Answers appear at the back of the book.*

Proverbs 16:3

_____ to the LORD whatever you do, and he will _____

your _____.

Proverbs 19:21

Many are the _____ in a person's _____, but it is the

_____ _____ that prevails.

Proverbs 21:5

The _____ of the diligent lead to _____ as surely as

_____ leads to _____.

Jeremiah 29:11

For I know the _____ I have for you," declares the _____,

"plans to _____ you and not to _____ you, plans to give

you _____ and a _____.

Ephesians 5:15—16

Be very _____ , then, how you _____ --not as

_____ but as wise, making the most of every _____ ,

because the days are _____.

Letters to **GOD.**

Dear God,

My day definitely got better. Miss Margaret didn't make me eat tuna casserole and didn't mind that I wanted a bowl of cereal instead. She laughed and said she didn't like tuna casserole either. After I helped with the dishes, we had a bowl of ice cream. YUM!

Once my little brother went to bed, Miss Margaret grabbed her bag of knitting supplies and asked me to join her on the couch so she could show me how to knit. I'm glad she had an extra pair of knitting needles just for me. She taught me how to put the yarn on the needle (called casting on), as well as how to make the knit stitch. In a couple of weeks when my scarf is as long as I want it to be, Miss Margaret is going to show me how to end the scarf or cast off. I didn't think I'd be able to learn so quickly, but I was able to get pretty far in just one night. Miss Margaret said I was a natural at knitting. She showed me a book with all kinds of things I could make once I'm really good at it. I wonder if she'd teach me how to make a sweater.

Next time my mom is working and my dad has a meeting, I'm going to ask Mom to call Miss Margaret. She's one cool lady!

And know what? I decided I'm not going to compare my life with Sydney's or anyone else's and to do my best with the life YOU have given me.

Thanks for everything, God, especially my new yarn!

Love,
Kaitlyn

Jot it down

Now, it's your turn. Write your own letter to God.

_____

_____

_____

_____

_____

_____

_____

_____

_____

_____

_____

_____

_____

"For I know the plans I have for you," declares the LORD,
"plans to prosper you and not to harm you, plans to give
you hope and a future."

Jeremiah 29:11

Make it!

Life Collage

A *collage* is an art technique in which you glue various materials to one solid surface. As you make this collage, do your best to create a piece of art that shows how grateful you are for the life God gave you.

What You Need:

* Poster board or colored construction paper

* Photos (or copies of photos)

* Magazines

* Markers or crayons

* Elmers glue or glue stick

* Optional decorations, such as: ribbons, beads, cut out shapes from tissue paper or feathers. Be creative with what you have at home.

What To Do:

* Design and color the poster board (or use construction paper) that you will use as a base.

* Add decorations to the background, if you wish.

* Use scissors to cut out images and words in various shapes from magazines to represent your life.

* Arrange magazine cutouts and photos on the poster board. Overlap them for an interesting look.

* Glue each item to the base.

* Allow time to dry.

* Hang your collage on your wall.

Write down the memory verse from the beginning of the chapter. Memorize it. How can you press on toward the goal to win the prize?

_____

_____

_____

_____

Keep running the race God has for you by doing and being your BEST.

Dear God, thank you for your many blessings. Help me to keep going when life gets tough. In Jesus' name, Amen.

* Chapter 2 *
All in the Family

Honor your father and your mother, so that you may live long in the land the LORD your God is giving you.

Exodus 20:12

Sarah's Dad

Sarah sat on the bench on the far side of the field with her gloved hands tucked under her thighs. Of all the days to get caught telling a lie, today was not a good day. Her chin quivered as she watched her frosty breath. Sarah spotted Amanda and her eyes narrowed.

Why did she have to tell?

Sarah shook her head in frustration as she made footprints in the snow to pass the time. She made a butterfly by twisting her feet this way and that. Sarah wished she were that butterfly so that she could fly away. She didn't want her mom to find out she received a warning slip for pushing her friend down in the snow.

The sound of the school bell brought a satisfying smile to Sarah's face. She jumped up from the bench and ran toward her classroom.

"Hey Sarah," called Amanda. "Wait up."

Sarah glanced over her shoulder and saw Amanda chase after her. She picked up her speed. No way was she going to talk to Amanda.

"Sarah," called Amanda once again. "Please stop."

In her rush, Sarah's knitted hat flew off her head, landing on the snow-packed ground. She quickly picked it up and put it back on before peeking over her shoulder once again. Amanda was gaining on her.

"Sarah, wait," called Amanda for the third time. "I want to tell you something."

Sarah slowed her steps and eventually stopped, her breath coming out in smoky puffs. "What do you want?" She planted her gloved hands on her hips.

Amanda caught up, breathing rapidly, and clutching her sides. "You're fast."

"Is that all you have to say?" Sarah turned around to head into class.

"No." Amanda stopped her with a hand. "Just listen, okay?"

Sarah tapped her foot. "I'm waiting."

"How long have we been friends?"

"We *were* friends for five years," said Sarah. "Why did you tell on me?"

"Because," said Amanda, "I don't want you to lie anymore."

Sarah folded her arms across her chest. "You know I'm just having a little fun. It's not like I'm hurting anyone."

"Yes, you are," said Amanda. "You can't go around telling people your dad works for the FBI."

"Why not?" Sarah's eyes narrowed.

"Because it's not true." Amanda softened her tone. "Your dad will get out of jail soon, won't he?"

"Shhh. I don't know. Just leave me alone." Sarah turned and walked straight into class, leaving Amanda standing in the snow.

Sarah had a hard time concentrating during math class. Her answers seemed all jumbled up as she tried to work the problems. She was startled when Mrs. Hughes placed a hand on her right shoulder, and said, "Sarah, will you please come with me?"

She shut her book and got up from her seat, following Mrs. Hughes out the door. Sarah's stomach knotted. She didn't look at anyone as she walked down the hall after the principal. Instead, she watched Mrs. Hughes's feet and listened to the clicking noise her heels made on the floor.

Why would the principal wear such fancy shoes on a snowy day? Sarah would've laughed out loud if she didn't see her mom walking into the school through the big front doors. Sarah's mouth felt like cotton. "Why is my mom here?"

"I asked her to come." Mrs. Hughes rested a hand on Sarah's shoulder. "We need to have a little talk."

Sarah hated the thought of having to talk with the principal *and* her mom at the same time. Moisture formed in her eyes and she blinked it away.

Mrs. Hughes greeted her mother. "Ladies, why don't we go have a seat in here." The principal opened the office door and pointed to some chairs.

"Sorry, Mom." Sarah didn't know exactly what Mrs. Hughes was going to say, but hoped her words would soften the blow.

Mom motioned for Sarah to go into the office first.

"Mrs. Murray, would you like some coffee?" the principal asked.

Mom shook her head. "No, thank you."

"Okay then, let's get started." Mrs. Hughes sat behind her desk. "Sarah, will you please tell your mom why you received a warning slip today."

Here we go, thought Sarah. "I shoved Amanda to the ground."

"Why did you do that?" Her mom's quiet tone matched her own.

"Because she was bugging me to tell people the truth about Dad." Sarah looked down at her boots, then back at her Mom.

"Oh, Sarah." Mom's forehead crinkled with concern.

"Kids keep asking me where he is. They say I don't really have a dad. I wanted them to think he was someone special so I told them he works for the FBI and is away on a secret mission." The words tumbled out as tears slid down her face.

Mrs. Hughes handed Sarah and her mom a tissue.

Sarah didn't want to cry, but the tears kept coming. She hiccupped and blew her nose, then looked over at her mom who gently swiped at her eyes.

"I'm sorry, Sarah," said Mom. "I know it's been hard."

"Your friend Amanda told the yard duty supervisor because she doesn't want you lying anymore about your father," said Mrs. Hughes. "I agree that if you told the truth, kids wouldn't tease you anymore."

"They'll laugh instead." Sarah folded her arms across her chest and lowered her eyes.

"Why don't we go home and talk about it?" Mom gathered Sarah in her arms. They walked to Sarah's classroom and collected her things before going home.

The car ride flew by in a white blur. Snow covered everything except where the cars had driven. That snow was dirty and black. It reminded Sarah of the song the worship leader had taught them at church last Sunday. She had said that when God forgives sin he washes us and makes us whiter than snow. Sarah knew lying was a sin. She didn't want to be like dirty snow, but clean like the white snow that falls from the sky. The bottom line was that she was ashamed of her father and didn't want others to know where he was. She realized now that by covering up the truth, she was making it worse.

"Mom," said Sarah once they pulled into their garage. "I'm not going to lie about Dad anymore. I don't like it that he's in jail, but it takes a lot more energy to keep up a lie."

After getting out of the car, Sarah's mom hugged her tight. "I'm glad, Sarah." Mom removed her boots. "You need to know that your father loves you very much. He made a bad choice and will be in jail for a little while longer, but it sounds like you are making a good choice. I'm proud of you."

"Thanks, Mom," said Sarah. "Can we make some hot chocolate? It's freezing outside."

What do YOU Think?

✱ Why did Sarah lie about her father? Do you think by making up a story it helped or hurt her? How?

_____

_____

_____

✱ Do you think Amanda did the right thing by telling a teacher? Why?

_____

_____

_____

＊How can making a good choice help you to honor your parents?

_____

_____

_____

·Tiny Tip· Every family goes through difficult times. A move, a new job, money issues, or relationship problems are some of the things that can put stress in the home. It's best to talk with your parents about how you feel. Your parents' job is to guide you through life's difficulties. And when you can't get the words out, remember God is only a prayer away.

Be joyful in hope, patient in affliction, faithful in prayer.
Romans 12:12

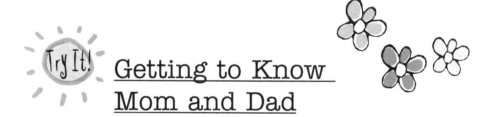

Try It! Getting to Know Mom and Dad

One of the best ways to know and understand your parents is by asking questions. By interviewing them, you'll gain clues to your family history and hear amazing stories. First, plan a time when there are no distractions. Turn off the television and don't answer the phone. Prepare a list of questions, or use the ones below to help the conversation flow.

Interview Hints:

- Ask questions that encourage more than a "yes" or "no" answer.
- Jot down some notes so that you'll remember what was said.
- Bring out old photo albums to get the conversation going.
- If your Mom or Dad is telling you a long story, be a good listener and don't interrupt.
- Interview your parents separately, and then share your notes.

- Another option is have them take turns answering around the dinner table. Or for a game show feel, call your family together, set up some chairs and play the host.

Interview Questions:

1. What is your earliest childhood memory?

2. How did your parents pick your name? Did you have a nickname?

3. What was your house like growing up? Did you have your own room?

4. What was your favorite television show when you were a kid? Favorite movie?

5. Did your family have special holiday traditions?

6. Tell me about your school friends.

7. Did you eat dinner together as a family? What was your favorite meal?

8. What was the most important thing you learned from your parents?

9. Describe your first date. Your wedding day.

10. What is the one thing you would like to be remembered for?

Idea: To dig deeper into your family history, ask your grandparents the same questions. You'll learn how much life has changed over the years.

Fun Facts about Life.

- How many people are in your family? _____

- How many animals do you have? _____ What are their names?

_____

• Do you live in the country, in a city, by the ocean, or nestled in the mountains? _____

_____

• Describe your house. _____

_____

_____

_____

• Where does your family like to go on vacation? _____

_____

• What games does your family like to play? _____

_____

• What are your grandparents' names? _____

_____

• Do they live nearby? How often do you see them? _____

_____

• How many cousins do you have? _____

• List their names and their ages. _____

_____

Did YOU Know? Parents are expected to discipline, teach, and provide for their children, while children are expected to cooperate, obey, and respect their parents. In order to honor your parents, you need to give them the recognition they deserve for their place in the family. By giving your parents respect, you place value on the gift God gave you.

Children, obey your parents in everything, for this pleases the Lord.

Colossians 3:20

REAL Life 101

FAMILY = God designed the family to consist of a father, a mother, and their children, but sometimes it doesn't work out that way. Some kids live in two homes, sharing time with their parents separately because of divorce. Other kids live with relatives, like grandparents or aunts and uncles. And sometimes kids live with foster parents because their birthparents are unable to care for them. Remember, God loves families and wants you to do your best in the one he gave **YOU**!

BIRTH ORDER is your position compared to your other siblings in the family. Have you ever wondered why your siblings say and do the things they do? Maybe your older sibling wants to boss you around, while your younger sibling always wants attention. Birth order plays a big part in how we relate to the people in our family, and affects who we are. Whether you are the oldest, middle, youngest, or only child, learning about  birth order is a fun way to look at yourself and how you get along with the people around you.

Experts have studied the topic for years and have come up with certain personality traits that are typical for a specific birth order. But remember, you are an individual and no one fits perfectly into a mold. Birth order gets more complicated when there is a family member with disabilities, adopted children in the family, or there are children from different parents.

Are you a . . .

First-Born:

The first-born child in the family is usually showered with attention, has tons of photos taken, and is a natural born leader. They tend to be confident, determined and organized, as well as easy to please and dependable. On the downside, parents may be stricter and expect more of a first-born.

Middle:

A middle child is used to sharing the attention, has fewer photos in the family albums, and is more calm and laid back. They tend to handle disappointments better than first-borns and are great at negotiating what they want. Middle children tend to make friends easily and are loyal through and through. On the downside, they may feel left out and misunderstood.

Youngest:

The youngest child, also known as "the baby" of the family, loves to be the center of attention, and enjoys making people laugh. They are persistent, great at telling stories, and have plenty of hugs to share. On the downside, they may feel their parents don't give them enough praise and treat them as younger than they are.

Only Child:

An only child doesn't have to share the attention, or anything else in the house. They are known to spend a lot of time with adults and can usually carry on a long conversation. They tend to be confident, organized, and do well in school. On the downside, they have a difficult time sharing their things and can be lonely.

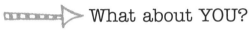 What about YOU?

✳ Are you the oldest, middle, youngest or only child? _____

_____

✳ What personality traits listed describe you? _____

_____

✳ How are you different from the descriptions? _____

_____

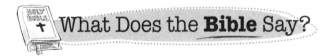 What Does the **Bible** Say?

Families are important to God. When you ask Jesus into your heart, you are adopted into his family. Ephesians 1:4-5 says, "For he chose us in him before the creation of the world to be holy and blameless in his sight. In love he predestined us for adoption to sonship through Jesus Christ, in accordance with his pleasure and will."

<u>Use the space below to draw</u>
<u>a picture of your family.</u>

# Letters to **GOD.**

Hi God,

Mom made spaghetti for dinner to cheer me up. She surprised me by poking the hard spaghetti noodles through the sausages before boiling— making it look like the noodles magically wove their way through while they cooked. SUPER COOL! She also made her special sauce with mushrooms, onions, and diced tomatoes. Even my older brother Tim got in the action. He cut the French bread and slathered it with butter and garlic, then wrapped it in tinfoil and put it in the oven. I set the table while Brooke, my little sister, colored me a picture in the family room. What would I do without my family? Mom says that as long as we stick together, we'll be okay. She also told me that every family goes through hard times.

After dinner Amanda called. She wondered why I left school early and hoped it wasn't because I pushed her down in the snow. I know she really cares about me even though it didn't seem like it earlier. We made plans to hang out on Saturday. Amanda doesn't have any brothers or sisters and gets lonely. Sometimes I feel left out at my house. Tim is always busy playing sports and Brooke demands my mom's attention all the time. It's not always easy being a middle child, but most days it's okay—like today.

Mom really listened to me while we drank hot chocolate. She understands how hard it's been having Dad gone and why I don't want to tell people that he stole $1,000 from his boss to pay our bills. He's coming home in a couple of months. Yippee! I can't wait!

Well, it's been a long day and I'm T-I-R-E-D. Good night!

Love,
Sarah

Jot it down

Now, it's your turn. Write your own letter about how God took care of your family during a difficult time.

_____

_____

_____

_____

_____

_____

_____

_____

_____

_____

_____

_____

_____

_____

_____

Cast all your anxiety on him because he cares for you.

1 Peter 5:7

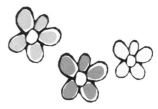

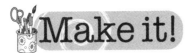

Character Mobile

Each person in your family is important and plays a role in making it all work. Individual members living under one roof can be a grandparent, parent, stepparent, child, sibling, or grandchild. As you think about each member in your family, consider creating this character mobile to thank God for the family he gave you.

What You Need:

* Wire hanger

* Cardstock and construction paper

* Hole punch

* Yarn, cut in various lengths from 6″ to 10″

* Scissors

* Colored pencils or markers

What To Do:

* On a large piece of paper, draw a picture of each of your family members. Don't forget your pets! Color. (Option: If you have a camera, take a photo of your family and print it out.)

* Cut each family member's picture out with your scissors.

* On the back of the cards write descriptive words for each person/animal in your family, such as loving, joyful, peaceful, kind, gentle, wise, helpful, etc.

* Hang the cards by punching a hole in each, tying them with different lengths of yarn, and attaching them to a wire hanger.

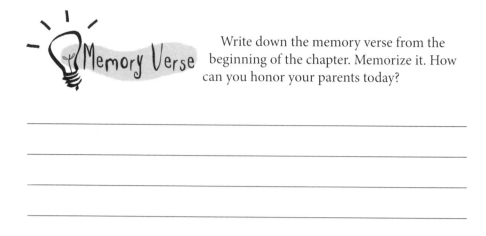

Write down the memory verse from the beginning of the chapter. Memorize it. How can you honor your parents today?

_____

_____

_____

_____

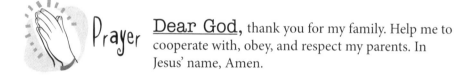

Whether you are a first-born, middle, youngest, or only child, you are UNIQUE and have an important role in your family.

Prayer **Dear God,** thank you for my family. Help me to cooperate with, obey, and respect my parents. In Jesus' name, Amen.

✳ Chapter 3 ✳
We're Best Friends, Aren't We?

My command is this: Love each other as I have loved you.
Greater love has no one than this: to lay down
one's life for one's friends.

John 15:12-13

Josie's Friend

Josie stared at the piece of paper in her hand. All the students in her class had received an orange piece of paper with the "Beautify our School" theme plastered at the top along with a list of jobs for the upcoming workday on Saturday. The plan was for the students to bring their parents to give their support through hard work. Money would also be collected for new sports equipment. Josie folded the piece of paper and stuck it into her backpack, then wandered down the hall to her brother's room.

"Hey Marcus, what're you doing?" Josie plopped onto her teenaged brother's beanbag chair.

"Not much. Just trying to get my homework done." Marcus sat at his desk and focused on his paper.

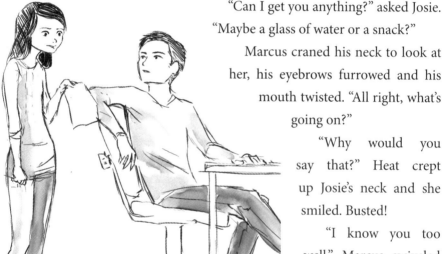

"Can I get you anything?" asked Josie. "Maybe a glass of water or a snack?"

Marcus craned his neck to look at her, his eyebrows furrowed and his mouth twisted. "All right, what's going on?"

"Why would you say that?" Heat crept up Josie's neck and she smiled. Busted!

"I know you too well." Marcus swiveled his chair around to face his sister. "You never offer to get me a snack unless you need something. So what's it this time?"

Josie fidgeted with the hem of her shirt. "You might not understand. But, then again—"

"Come right out and say it," Marcus said.

"Wait here. I'll be right back." Josie ran down the hall to her room. A minute later she stood by Marcus and handed him the orange piece of paper. "Read this."

Josie bit her lower lip as her brother read.

Marcus looked up at her. "What's the problem? Looks like it would be fun to paint a few benches or pull some weeds with your friends."

Josie placed her hands on her hips. "Did you notice the date of the workday?"

Marcus looked down at the piece of paper. "Oh, it's this Saturday."

"Yeah. *This* Saturday. Mom and Dad can't be at two places at once. How are they going to pick between your last soccer game and an important workday for the school?"

"That's easy." Marcus leaned back in his chair with his hands behind his head. "Of course they'll come to my game. There will be other workdays at school, and besides you don't want to work on a Saturday when you can have fun watching your brother play his last soccer game of the season."

"But . . . wait a minute. Why don't we let Mom and Dad decide? I just wanted you to know." Josie grabbed the piece of paper. "See ya. Happy studying." She took off in the direction of her bedroom not wanting to look back at the face she was sure her brother was making.

Once in her bedroom, she pulled out another piece of paper from her backpack. The once sealed envelope had been stuffed inside her history book. She looked at the hand-written letter her teacher wrote to her parents.

> *Dear Mr. and Mrs. Rodriguez,*
>
> *As per our phone conversation, Josie's classmates have voted her onto the Student Council. Her participation this Saturday is crucial to show her commitment for the school. Please let me know if you will be able to join her this Saturday for "Beautify our School" day.*
>
> *Sincerely,*
>
> *Mrs. Peters*

Josie shoved the letter and the orange piece of paper back inside her backpack. She tried to make sense of the thoughts that raced around in her head. She had thought she wanted to be on Student Council, but now she wasn't so sure. Josie had to admit the main reason she decided to add her name to the possible candidates was because her best friend Chelsea was already on the list. Chelsea told her that two people from each class would get voted in. Josie was sure they both would be on Student Council together. She won but Chelsea did not. Robert slipped his name in at the very last moment and landed the other spot. To make matters worse, Chelsea didn't talk to her the rest of the day.

And now, with her brother's last soccer game this weekend, her parents would be torn. Josie didn't know what to do. A knock on her door made her jump. "Come in."

"Josie, Marcus told me you had something to show me¬—an orange piece of paper with school information on it?" asked Mom. "What's that all about?"

Marcus doesn't waste any time. "I was going to show you when Dad came home." She reached inside her backpack and pulled out the paper and the teacher's note, and handed them to her mom. "Here it is."

Her mom looked at the papers. "It's important for you go to the school on Saturday."

"I wish I didn't get voted on Student Council!" Josie blurted. "It's one thing choosing to go on Saturday, but I'm being forced to go. And another thing, I think my friendship with Chelsea is ruined!" Josie flopped down on her bed and buried her face in the pillow.

Mom rubbed Josie's back. "Where did all this come from? You should feel honored to be voted on Student Council. Chelsea will come around. Why don't you call her and ask if she'd like to go with you this Saturday?"

Josie turned to face her mom, leaning on an elbow. "Do you think she'll be friends with me again? I didn't mean to get on Student Council without her. It was her idea in the first place."

"Of course, she'll be your friend. You two have been close since you were babies. I think she's just disappointed right now." Her mom pushed a strand of hair behind Josie's ear. "Can I ask you something?"

"Sure," said Josie.

"Did you really want to be on Student Council?"

Josie sat up and wrapped her arms around her knees. "You know, I did. I was just scared I wouldn't get enough votes. I do have some really good ideas on how to improve our school. I just wish Chelsea and I could have done it together."

Mom nodded. "Why don't you make that phone call now?"

"All right." Josie sprang from her bed and darted down the hall. When she approached the phone, butterflies flitted around in her stomach. She pushed down the lump that had formed in her throat, and reached for the phone. She punched in her friend's number and waited until the third ring before someone picked up.

"Hello."

"Hi, Chelsea? This is Josie."

"Oh, hi." Chelsea's voice sounded low and sad.

Josie paced the floor and rubbed her sweaty palm down the side of her jeans. "I'm wondering if you want to go to the 'Beautify your School' day this Saturday?"

"Are you trying to rub it in that I didn't make Student Council?" Chelsea's tone held a hint of anger.

"No."

"Then why do you want me to come?"

"Because you're my best friend." Josie's voice softened. "I'm really bummed that we didn't make Student Council together. In fact, I'd rather not be in Student Council at all if it means we're not going to be friends."

"Really?" asked Chelsea. "You'd do that for me?"

"If you wanted me to," said Josie.

"Wow," said Chelsea. "You're a good friend."

"Thanks." Josie grinned from the compliment. Then, a thought jarred her. What had she done? "But, you don't really want me to quit do you? Because I've never been voted in for something before. What am I going to say to our teacher, or the class, or my parents?"

"Okay, okay, stop talking." Chelsea giggled. "Of course I don't want you to quit. Just the thought that you would is good enough for me."

Josie sighed with relief. "Thanks."

"By the way, I'd love a ride with you this Saturday. My parents are going to my sister's ballet recital and they don't want to miss it."

Oh no, Marcus! "I forgot about my brother's soccer game," said Josie. "My parents love watching him play, especially because his team has never lost a game. They'll probably end up flipping a coin."

"I guess this will be your first debate on Student Council," said Chelsea.

"Duty calls," said Josie. "I'm glad you're still my best friend. See you tomorrow."

What do YOU Think?

✱ Have you ever been voted for or picked for a team without your best friend? How did that make you feel?

_____

_____

_____

✱ How did Chelsea respond when Josie told her that she would rather not be on Student Council if it meant they weren't going to be friends?

_____

_____

_____

✱ What can you do to show your friends how much you care?

_____

_____

_____

·Tiny Tip· Laying down your life for a friend does not mean that you have to die for them. It does mean, however, that you'll be a *true friend,* someone who looks out for and wants the best for someone special in your life.

A friend loves at all times, and a brother is born for a time of adversity.
Proverbs 17:17

Friendship Quiz

Have you ever heard the saying "true-blue friend?" It means having someone who is loyal to you. Take this quiz and find out what kind of friend YOU are. Circle one answer for each situation.

What would you do?

1. Your friend is invited to a party and you weren't. Would you:
   A. Ask her not to go.
   B. Invite her to your house on that day.
   C. Tell her she's a good friend and you're not surprised she was invited.

2. Do you know what your best friend's favorite color, food, and television show are?
   A. No. You don't pay attention to such minor details.
   B. Maybe, but you need to ask to make sure.
   C. Yes! And you could list them off right now.

3. If your friend did something embarrassing, would you:
   A. Turn around and walk away. You don't want to draw attention to the situation.
   B. Laugh. It will help lighten the mood.
   C. Help her. There's nothing worse than being embarrassed.

4. Would you play a game you didn't like just to hang out with your friend?
   A. No way. If she were such a good friend she wouldn't ask you to play.
   B. Yes, as long as she does what you like to do next.
   C. Sure. Any amount of time spent being with her is fun.

5. Someone is bullying your friend. Would you:
   A. Ignore the situation. The bully isn't worth your time.
   B. Step in and defend her without thinking about the consequences.
   C. Tell an adult who can handle the situation better than you.

6. If your friend did something you know is wrong, would you:
   A. Cover it up so that no one notices.
   B. Let it go. We all make mistakes.
   C. Confront her and encourage her to make things right.

7. Your friend is sick and can't come to school. Do you:
   A. Sit alone during lunch and feel sorry for yourself.
   B. Hang out with some other girls without giving your sick friend another thought.
   C. Make her a "Get Well" card and collect her homework.

8. It's Saturday night and your friend asks you to sleep over. Do you:
   A. Call your mom and beg her to let you stay. She can pick you up after church. Your friend doesn't go to church so why should you?
   B. Sleep over, but make sure your mom or dad picks you up in time for church. You want to set a good example.
   C. Spend the night, but ask your friend if she'd like to go to church with your family on Sunday morning.

9. At school your friend hands you a note and asks you to meet her in the bathroom. She's clearly upset, but you don't know why. You:
   A. Stay in class until the bell rings. Your friend is a drama queen and it's not worth getting in trouble.
   B. Sneak out of class with her. Your friend is more important than school.
   C. Ask the teacher if you can have a few minutes alone with your friend to find out what's the matter.

10. You're shopping at the mall with your friend and you both like the same shirt. Do you:
    A. Tell her she can buy it, then go back to the mall and buy one for your self.
    B. Flip a coin. May the best person win!
    C. Agree to be twins. It's fun to wear the same clothes as your best friend.

Count how many times you circled each letter and write it down.

A: _____

B: _____

C: _____

If you circled mostly A's: Beware! You're only thinking of yourself. Consider putting others first. In order to have a true friend, you need to be one.

If you circled mostly B's: Your intentions may be good, but you're not quite there. Challenge yourself to be the best friend you can be.

If you circled mostly C's: Congratulations, you are a true friend! You are kind, aren't afraid to do the right thing when the need arises, and don't mind sharing your friend with others. Way to go!

Fun Facts about Life.

Fill in the blanks:

✳ My best friend's name is _____

✳ Describe what she looks like. _____

_____

_____

✳ Her favorite color is _____

✳ Her favorite food is _____

✳ Her favorite movie is _____

✳ Her favorite song is _____

✳ What sport does she play? _____

* Is her room clean or messy? _____

* What do you like to do together? _____

* Does she collect anything or have a hobby? _____

_____

* If she were an animal, what would she be? _____

* If she were in a movie, what part would she play? _____

_____

* What would her dream job be? _____

_____

* Are her ears pierced? _____ Does she wear a ring? _____

* Would she rather get up early or go to bed late? _____

Ask your friend
these questions
and see if your
answers are correct.

Did **YOU** Know?

It's okay to have more than one friend.
In fact, it's normal. You can have close friends
at school, church, and at home. Yes, even a sibling can be one of your best
friends! Different people have different personalities and you can enjoy
spending time with more than one person. And remember, God can be one of
your best friends, too!

Come near to God and he will come near to you.

James 4:8

REAL Life 101

FRIEND = a person you know, like, and trust, and who genuinely cares about what happens in your LIFE!

As a Christian girl, it's important to find friends who have the same values as you do. There will be times when you'll need to make decisions and choices that reflect what it means to follow God and you don't want to place yourself in situations you don't want to be in. Picking the right type of friends is important. So how do you go about doing that?

Consider these guidelines when choosing people you want to hang out with:

- **It is better to be alone than to be in the wrong crowd.** Listen to the way they talk. Do they cut people down? What do they like to do? If they make fun of other kids or constantly get in trouble, separate yourself from them. You want to be far away from people who will pressure you into making bad choices.

- **Find friends with similar interests.** Do you play on a sports team? Go to a youth group at church? Take dance lessons? Liking the same activities is important to building a friendship and giving you stuff to talk about.

- **Look for personalities that complement your own.** She doesn't need to be exactly like you, but it's nice when you can talk about serious issues or laugh at the same jokes.

- **Ask questions.** When you want to become friends with someone, ask questions. Find out who she is and what makes her tick. It shows that you care and opens the door to friendship.

• **Friendship is a two-way street.** Choose a friend who gives as much to your friendship as you do. It's not fun to feel like you're the only one who wants to be friends.

• **Positive people make the best friends.** A sure sign to know if you should be friends with someone is whether you feel good about yourself when you are around her. If not, find another friend.

• **True friendship takes time.** Don't rush to tell someone your biggest secret. Wait until you know you can trust her. If she genuinely cares about you, she'll be your friend for years.

• **Don't forget your family.** As you gain your identity and independence, remember your family comes first above friends. Your parents and siblings will always be in your life, while friendships may come and go.

• **How does she feel about God?** If she believes in God the same way you do, chances are she'll make good choices and be a good influence on you. When parents teach their daughters values and morals from the Bible, they will be able to know right from wrong.

• **No friend is perfect!** Everyone makes mistakes from time to time—you included. Best friends weather the storms of life and forgive one another.

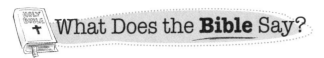

What Does the **Bible** Say?

The Bible gives us clear examples of good and bad friends.   Fill in the blanks to match the person with their description. Highlight the capitalized words (pink for good and yellow for bad), and learn from what they did. *Answers appear at the back of the book.*

Elisha   **Judas**

Pharaoh's cupbearer   **Jonathan**

Ruth   **Ahithophel**

Paul

She was **LOYAL** even during difficult times. When Naomi told her to stay

behind, _____ said, "Where you go, I will go, and where you stay I

will stay. Your people will be my people and your God my God." (Ruth 1:16)

When King Saul wanted to kill David, _____ **SAVED**

David's life. He told David, "Whatever you want me to do, I'll do it for you."

(1 Samuel 20:4)

As King David's trusted counselor, _____**BETRAYED**

King David by befriending an enemy who wanted to overthrow the kingdom.

_____ also gave the king bad advice and spread rumors about

the king. (2 Samuel 15:12—17:23)

_____ **STUCK BY** Elijah by not letting Elijah go to Bethel alone. He said, 'As surely as the Lᴏʀᴅ lives and as you live, I will not leave you.' So they went down to Bethel." (2 Kings 2:2)

_____ was in prison with Joseph and had a dream. Joseph interpreted his dream, telling him that in three days time he'd be released from prison. Instead of showing Joseph kindness, he **FORGOT** about him. (Genesis 40:1-23)

_____ helped people grow in their faith by **ENCOURAGING** them and being bold to **CORRECT** them. (1 Corinthians 1:1-9)

As one of Jesus' disciples, _____ acted like a friend but he put his **GREED** above everything else and accepted thirty pieces of silver to betray Jesus. (Matthew 26:14-15)

Letters to **GOD.**

Dear God,

Dad came with me to "Beautify our School" day. He brought along a few potted plants, soil, and a shovel. Mrs. Peters was so grateful for my dad's donation, and Chelsea and I helped him plant the flowers next to the school sign. It sure looks nice!

When Robert (the boy who took Chelsea's spot on Student Council) showed up, Chelsea started acting funny. She wouldn't talk to me and started picking up trash on the far side of the field. At first I was angry. Why couldn't she just get over it? It wasn't like I planned on getting on Student Council without her!

That's when I heard a couple of girls talking about how Chelsea only thinks about herself and that it served her right for not making it. Can you believe that? Well, I wasn't going to stand around and listen to a bunch of mean girls talk about my friend that way! I was about to march right up to them and tell them exactly what I thought, but decided against it. There had to be a better way to show them they were wrong.

I grabbed a large trash bag and went over to where Chelsea was working. I could tell she didn't want me near, but I opened my trash bag and suggested we work together. Then I asked her to share some of her ideas for improving our school. She looked shocked! I told her that just because she wasn't on Student Council didn't mean that she didn't have a say. Later that afternoon I made a point of telling the other girls what GREAT ideas my friend has. By the end of the day, everyone agreed!

Love,
   Josie

Jot it down

Now, it's your turn. Write your own letter to God and tell him about a time you helped a friend in need.

_____

_____

_____

_____

_____

_____

_____

_____

_____

_____

_____

_____

_____

_____

One who has unreliable friends soon comes to ruin, but there is a friend who sticks closer than a brother.

Proverbs 18:24

Make it!

Beaded Friendship Bracelet

While making this bracelet, think of ways you can be a better friend.

What You Need:

* Yarn

* Large beads

* Masking tape

* Scissors

* Ruler

What To Do:

1. Wrap a strand of yarn around your wrist. Add three inches and cut. Measure and cut two more strands that are twice as long as your first piece.

2. Hold the strands together, matching up the edges on one side. Tie a knot.

3. Tape the knotted end to a solid surface like a table, for example.

4. Separate the strands. With the shortest piece in the middle, thread as many beads as it takes to fill it up, leaving about an inch at the end. Tape to the table.

5. With the longer pieces, tie a knot between the beads by making sure one strand goes on top of the middle strand and one goes underneath. Continue making knots between each bead.

6. When you come to the end, undo the tape and tie all the ends together. Snip any extra yarn so that all the edges are even.

7. Give the bracelet to your best friend! Then make one for yourself.

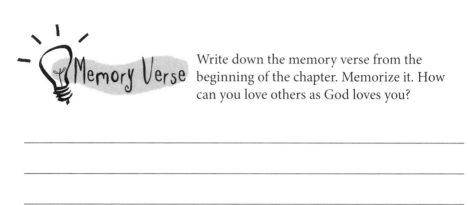 Write down the memory verse from the beginning of the chapter. Memorize it. How can you love others as God loves you?

_____

_____

_____

In order to have a true friend, you need to be one.

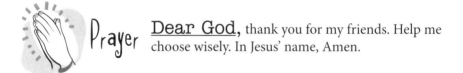 **Prayer** __Dear God,__ thank you for my friends. Help me choose wisely. In Jesus' name, Amen.

* Chapter 4 *
Boy Crazy!

So God created human beings in his own likeness,
He created them to be like himself.
He created them as male and female.

Genesis 1:27

Elizabeth's Crush

"There he is," Elizabeth whispered into her friend's ear. "Isn't Zachary cute?"

"So that's the new boy, huh?" Hannah leaned back against the lockers. "Where'd you say he was from?"

"Texas. You should hear him talk. I could listen to him all day." Elizabeth smiled.

"My cousin lives in Texas," said Hannah. "Does Zachary say *y'all?*"

"I'm sure he does. Doesn't everyone from Texas say that?"

"All I know is I went to visit my cousin for two weeks last summer and before I knew it I was talking just like her—"

"Shh. Here he comes." Elizabeth tucked her hair behind her ear and pretended she needed something from her locker.

"Hi." Hannah waved.

"Hey." The new boy tipped his head back and grinned, then kept walking.

Elizabeth slumped. There went her opportunity. Why didn't she have the guts to say something? If she didn't talk to him, he'd like Hannah instead. Of course, Hannah was the prettiest girl in the class. What boy didn't like her?

Hannah's brows lowered. "You missed your chance."

"I didn't know what to say." Elizabeth shrugged a shoulder. "It would've sounded dumb if I said hi, too."

"So instead you wimped out. Boys aren't that scary."

"I don't have an older brother, like you. There're only girls in my house. Even my dog's a girl."

Hannah cocked her head. "What about your dad?"

Elizabeth sighed. "That's true, but I only see him every other weekend."

"Come on, let's get to class. The bell's about to ring." Hannah looped her arm around Elizabeth's and tugged her down the hall.

All during science, Elizabeth kept glancing at Zachary a few rows to her left. She liked how tall he was and the way his hair touched the collar of his shirt. He had nice green eyes too. Her heartbeat quickened and she had an odd sensation in the pit of her stomach. Is this what love felt like? A smile spread across her face.

Mrs. Michaels walked up to her desk, catching her staring at Zachary. *How embarrassing!*

"Elizabeth? What's your answer?"

She might have a clue what to say if she knew the question. Elizabeth shook her head. "I don't know." A few giggles erupted. Was it her imagination or was the whole class looking at her? She wanted to crawl under her desk.

"I asked you what color your parents eyes were. We're discussing how the genes received from one's parents determines what eye color you will have."

No wonder she was thinking of Zachary's green eyes. She wanted to disappear. "Well?" asked Mrs. Michaels.

If she didn't answer quickly the whole class, including Zachary, would think she was dense, and that's the last thing she wanted. "My mom's eyes are blue and my dad's are brown." There, she said it. She stole a quick glimpse at the boy with the Texas drawl. Zachary grinned and winked at her. *He actually winked!* Elizabeth bit her lower lip and took a deep breath. Could Zachary actually like her too? The thought made her palms sweat.

Mrs. Michaels continued. "And what color are your eyes?"

She better pay attention. "Blue."

Her teacher went on to explain how if both parents have a blue and brown gene, their child's eyes will be brown, but if the child inherits the blue gene from each parent then the child will have blue eyes. If the child only inherits one blue gene then they will have brown eyes. Sounded complicated. Mrs. Michaels ambled back to the front of the room and grabbed a stack of papers. "This diagram will help explain."

The pile of papers made its way around the room.

"For tonight's homework, I would like you to look closely at your eyes in the mirror. You might be surprised by what you see. Then draw and color a picture of your eye on an eight by eleven sheet of paper."

The bell rang. The students gathered their things and shoved them in their backpacks before scurrying off to the lunchroom.

Hannah caught up with Elizabeth. "Let's sit by Zachary. I saw him looking at you in class."

"He did more than that," Elizabeth sighed. "He winked at me."

"You sure he didn't have something in his eye?" Was Hannah jealous?

Elizabeth pulled her shoulders back. "I'm positive. He winked . . . and smiled."

Hannah raised her brows. "Now that's a new development." The sour attitude was replaced with a grin.

"If we do sit by Zachary," said Elizabeth, "can you please make sure I don't make a fool of myself? I don't want to ruin everything."

"Just be yourself," said Hannah.

"That's what I'm afraid of. He might find out how goofy I am and run the other way."

"If he does, then he's not worth it," Hannah said.

"How do you make friends so easily with boys? You seem to be able to talk to them with no problem."

"Let me give you a little hint," said Hannah. "My mom told me that at our age it's better to be friends. There's no pressure that way and you won't need to be someone you're not."

"Makes sense," said Elizabeth. "But I still want him to like me."

"But you don't even know him," said Hannah. "Yeah, he's cute, but what if he's mean or rude? Would you like him then?"

"Probably not. How come you know so much anyway?"

"I have an older brother, remember? Plus, my mom and I talk a lot. Oh, one more thing. She said boys mature a lot slower than girls."

"What does that mean?" asked Elizabeth.

"Something about taking longer to grow up," said Hannah.

Elizabeth felt a tap on her shoulder. She turned to look, but no one was there. Elizabeth twisted her neck the other direction. Zachary grinned at her.

"My point exactly," whispered Hannah.

"Are you going to the lunchroom?" asked Zachary.

Elizabeth found her voice. "Yeah, are you?"

"Uh-huh," said Zachary. "Want to sit together?"

"Sure." Elizabeth smiled.

His eyes were definitely a nice shade of green.

What do YOU Think?

✻ Is there a boy at school or church that you like? What makes him special?

_____

_____

_____

✻ Why did Elizabeth like Zachary? Does she know him very well?

_____

_____

_____

* What advice about boys would you give Elizabeth if you were her friend?

_____

_____

_____

Just because girls act boy crazy doesn't mean they really are. They might just be pretending in order to fit in. It's best to wait for boy/girl relationships until you're older and better equipped to handle the changes it brings.

> *There is a time for everything, and a season*
> *for every activity under the heavens.*
> Ecclesiastes 3:1

Try It! How Boy Crazy Are You?

Every girl goes through a phase when she thinks about boys all the time. It's not surprising since movies, television, music, magazines, and even friends can sway you in this direction. Take this quiz to find out what effect boys have on you. Circle one answer for each question.

What would you do?

1. If you could spend the day with anyone on the planet, who would it be?
   A. My girl friends.
   B. My best friend, who happens to be a guy.
   C. As many guys as possible.
   D. My boyfriend, or would-be boyfriend if my parents would let me date!

2. How many crushes have you had this past year?
A. None.
B. I have lots of guy friends. I don't consider them crushes.
C. One. And I hope he likes me too.
D. Too many to count!

3. When listening to music, do you have a certain song for the boy you like?
A. No. I like a lot of songs, and none of them remind me of a guy.
B. I have a song for *every* boy I like.
C. YES! Every time I hear it.
D. It changes from year to year.

4. Why do you go to school activities or church youth group?
A. To hang out with friends AND cute guys.
B. My crush is there, of course.
C. Because it's fun.
D. I've gone for a boy in the past, but it's rare.

5. How many times a day do you talk about boys?
A. I only talk about one boy, but I mention him a lot.
B. It depends on which friends I hang out with. If they talk about boys, then I do too.
C. Maybe once or twice depending on the situation.
D. When do I not talk about boys?

You are TOTALLY boy crazy if you chose:

1. c.

2. d.

3. b.

4. a.

5. d.

Be careful! You don't want to grow up too fast. You have plenty of time to learn about boys.

You are SOMEWHAT boy crazy if you chose:

1. d.

2. c.

3. c.

4. b.

5. a.

So you have a secret crush, huh? It's okay as long as you don't put all your hopes and dreams into having a relationship with him. There's so much more to life.

You are <u>BARELY</u> boy crazy if you chose:

1. b.

2. b.

3. d.

4. d.

5. b.

You have a healthy view of boys and don't let the world revolve around them. Good for you! Be careful, however, about repeating past mistakes or letting your friends pull you in a direction you don't want to go.

You are <u>NOT AT ALL</u> boy crazy if you chose:

1. a.

2. a.

3. a.

4. c.

5. c.

You're not ready to think about boys and that's perfectly okay! In fact, it's GREAT! At this point, it makes life less complicated. Congratulations for being your own person.

Did **YOU** Know? During Bible times, girls were betrothed between 12 and 13 years of age and typically gave birth to their first child a year later. Mary, the mother of Jesus, was most likely 14 years old when she traveled to Bethlehem. Now, the average age for women to marry is closer to 30. What does that mean for you? Unless you were born during Bible times, the boy who catches your eye now is most likely not the person you'll marry.

Wait for the LORD; be strong, and take heart and wait for the LORD.

Psalm 27:14

REAL Life 101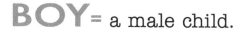

BOY = a male child.

Remember in preschool when you played with a boy and it was no big deal? Then when you started elementary school, you thought boys were gross and you only wanted to play with girls? Maybe you still think boys are disgusting. There will be a time when you are suddenly aware of boys and how they are different from girls. You might even have a secret crush. The best thing to do is focus on the friendship instead of a boyfriend/girlfriend relationship.

Here are some helpful hints:

- **It's not a big deal to talk to a boy, even though it might feel like it.** Follow the guidelines to making friends in the previous chapter and you'll have no problem choosing the right type of guy friends for you.

- **Boys and girls need to respect each other and have appropriate boundaries.** Ask your parents about this. They'll give you their thoughts about what's okay and what isn't, and when they think it's time to date. Don't be surprised if they say not until you're 16!

- **If you're not ready for a relationship and a boy asks you to be his girlfriend, be honest with him.** It's hard to tell him you'd rather be friends, but it's better to be truthful and let him down gently than let him hope for a relationship you're not ready for or don't want.

- **Sometimes girls want to impress boys so much that they allow themselves to be mistreated.** Inappropriate comments or bad behavior from boys is not acceptable and needs to be addressed. Girls that allow this type of behavior don't usually have a positive male figure in their lives and typically have low self-esteem. The best choice is to discuss what's going on with a caring adult.

- **Allow God, instead of the cute boy, to be number one in your life.** God teaches us about the kind of love he sees as important in 1 Corinthians 13:4-8, which says, "Love is patient, love is kind. It does not envy, it does not boast, it is not proud. It does not dishonor others, it is not self-seeking, it is not easily angered, it keeps no records of wrongs. Love does not delight in evil but rejoices with the truth. It always protects, always trusts, always hopes, always perseveres. Love never fails."

Fun Facts about Life.

Fill in the blanks:

＊How many boys live at your house? (Yes, your dad counts.) _____

＊If you have brothers, are they older or younger? _____

_____

＊What do you do when you hang out together? _____

_____

＊Name a guy friend. _____

＊Describe him. _____

_____

＊What does he like to talk about? _____

_____

＊What church does he attend? _____

_____

＊What is his favorite subject in school? _____

＊What are his hobbies? _____

＊How do you feel when you're around him? _____

_____

_____

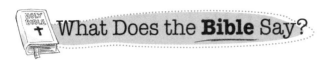

What Does the **Bible** Say?

Above everything, God wants you to have a relationship with HIM before you think about having a boyfriend. It's natural for boys and girls to want to hold hands, kiss, and eventually marry and have sex. But according to the Bible, God's plan is for you to keep things pure. For now, it's best to learn how to be a boy's friend.

Unscramble the words below and place them in the blank lines to discover the hidden message. *Answers appear at the back of the book.*

VILE   CAEPE

SSENSUOETHGIR   ORDL

HTIFA   RUPE

EOVL   RTHEA

Flee the _____desires of youth and pursue

_____, _____,

_____ and _____, along

with those who call on the _____ out of a _____

_____.   2 Timothy 2:22

 Letters to **GOD.**

Hi God,

At lunch today Zachary shared his grapes with me. It felt weird taking turns grabbing off the same vine, especially when our hands brushed against each other a few times. Suddenly I was uncomfortable with the whole idea of this boy-girl thing. Yeah, I know it's normal for me to notice boys, but I'm definitely not ready for anything but friendship! I know this will make my mom happy. I heard her talking with my older sister about how she can't go out with a boy until she's 16. I have a long way to go before I'm old enough, but that's okay.

Then when we were heading to class, Zachary's friend Tyler nudged me and wiggled his eyebrows. He told me that Zachary thinks I'm cute and wants to hang out with me *alone* some time. A shiver ran through me and not the good kind either. What type of guy would tell his friend something like that? Eww.

After school, Zachary wondered why I was acting funny. I told him what his friend Tyler said. He denied the part about hanging out alone, and instead asked if Hannah and I could come to his party. He said he was inviting the whole class. That didn't sound threatening. In fact, it sounded fun! Then when I got home from school, a thought zipped through my head. Zachary thought I was cute. Isn't that what all girls dream of? But Hannah was right. As much as I wanted Zachary to like me, at this point it was better to be friends.

Love,
            Elizabeth

P.S. I wonder if Mom will let me go to Zachary's party? Hope so!

Jot it down

Now, it's your turn. Write your own letter to God and tell Him about a time you liked a boy but decided it was better to be friends.

_____

_____

_____

_____

_____

_____

_____

_____

_____

_____

_____

_____

_____

_____

_____

Be devoted to one another in love.
Honor one another above yourselves.

Romans 12:10

Make it!

Friendship Frame

It's fun to take pictures of your friends and frame them on your wall. Try making this simple friendship frame to capture the guys and girls in your life.

What You Need:

* Inexpensive wood frame

* Paint

* Buttons or beads

* Glue

What To Do:

1. Take the glass out of an inexpensive wooden frame.

2. Paint the frame.

3. After the paint dries, glue buttons or beads around the edge of the frame.

4. Place a picture of you and your friends inside and replace the glass.

 Write down the memory verse from the beginning of the chapter. Memorize it. How did God create mankind?

_____

_____

_____

It's okay to like boys (that's the way God designed it), but it's best to be friends.

 **Dear God,** thank you for creating girls and boys. Help me to focus on a relationship with You most of all. In Jesus' name, Amen.

Chapter 5
Ups and Downs

Let the peace of Christ rule in your hearts, since as members
of one body you were called to peace. And be thankful.

Colossians 3:15

Lisa's Friend

"Your turn." Lisa threw the basketball to her friend Wendy.

"Thanks." Wendy caught the ball and turned to face the basketball hoop. "Watch this shot."

"Okay, show-off. Let's see it," Lisa teased. She shaded her eyes from the noonday sun and watched as Wendy threw the ball toward the hoop.

SWISH.

"Nice shot," said Lisa.

Wendy put her hands on her hips. "Your turn to make it from this spot, otherwise I win."

Lisa picked up the ball. "Can I throw granny-style? You know I can't make it from this far away."

"You're supposed to throw it exactly like I did, but since you're my best friend I'll let you throw it any way you want." Wendy grinned.

"Thanks." Lisa bounced it several times before looking up at the basketball hoop. She took a deep breath, and then threw the ball with all her might. It flew right over the top of the hoop. "Oops." Both girls looked at each other and laughed.

"I win!" Wendy pumped her fists.

Mrs. Taylor came outside. Her brows were drawn together and her mouth was turned down. "Girls, come here."

"What's up, Mom?" Wendy's eyes narrowed.

"Something terrible has happened." Mrs. Taylor wrapped her arms around her daughter. "Grandpa was working in his garden when Grandma spotted him slumped over. He had a heart attack."

"Is he okay?" asked Wendy.

"Grandma ran to him and checked to see if he was breathing or had a pulse." Mrs. Taylor shook her head. "Wendy, Grandpa died."

Tears formed in Wendy's eyes and spilled onto her cheeks. "No!" she screamed and ran into her house.

Lisa stood there not knowing what to do. She hugged the basketball to her chest and wished she were laughing like she had been moments ago. Now, her friend was crying from losing her grandpa and she stood like a frozen statue.

"Lisa, your mom is coming to get you. You and Wendy can have a sleepover another night. Okay?" Mrs. Taylor reached over and gave Lisa a hug. "Why don't you come into the house while you wait."

Would she see Wendy come out of her room before her mom arrived?

Lisa nodded, not knowing what to say. She followed Mrs. Taylor into the house, placed the basketball by the front door, and sat down at the kitchen table as Mrs. Taylor made some phone calls, including purchasing tickets for the next available flight to Montana. Lisa never had anyone die in her family and had a strange feeling in the pit of her stomach.

A knock sounded on the front door.

"I'll get it," said Lisa to Mrs. Taylor, who was still on the phone. She walked over to the front door and opened it. "Mom!" Lisa wrapped her arms around her mother. "I thought you'd never get here."

Mom hugged her tight. "Everything will be all right. How's Wendy doing?"

"It was awful. Wendy and I were having so much fun, and then Mrs. Taylor told us that her grandpa had a heart attack and died." Lisa pushed down the lump that had formed in her throat. "Wendy ran into the house, and I haven't seen her since."

"Why don't we see if there's anything we can do to help before we leave?" Lisa's mom removed her jacket and hung it on the coat rack.

"Are you sure we shouldn't just go?" Lisa tossed a glance toward the kitchen.

"We'll only stay a minute."

Lisa followed her mom into the kitchen. She watched as her mom embraced Mrs. Taylor.

I can do that.

She climbed the stairs to her friend's bedroom. With each step, Lisa's stomach twisted into a tight knot. She tried to imagine what it would be like finding out her grandpa had died. Tears formed in her eyes. When she came to Wendy's door, she drew in a deep breath and knocked.

"Who is it?" Wendy's voice sounded hoarse from crying.

"It's Lisa."

"Come in."

Lisa opened the door and found Wendy lying on her bed. She ran to her

friend and gave her a big hug. "I'm sorry about your grandpa."

"Thanks." Wendy smiled through her tears. "You always know what to say."

Lisa grabbed a tissue and handed it to Wendy. "I just tried to imagine what it would be like."

"I still can't believe it." Wendy sat up and blew her nose. "It doesn't feel real."

"I know, right?" Lisa shrugged her shoulders. "But it must be. Your mom bought airline tickets to Montana."

Wendy's eyes widened. "I've never been to a funeral before."

"Me, neither. You'll have to tell me all about it."

Wendy nodded. "Do you think we'll need to wear black?"

"I don't know," said Lisa. "Maybe they only do that in the movies."

"You're probably right."

"I'm going to miss you."

"Thanks," said Wendy. "I'm going to miss you, too."

"Lisa." Her mom quietly knocked on the door.

"Come in."

She opened the door, headed straight toward Wendy, and rested a hand on her shoulder. "I'm so sorry, sweetie. I know you're going to miss your grandpa a lot."

"Thanks." Wendy wrapped her arms around bent legs.

"Lisa, it's time to go. Wendy and her family need to pack. Their flight leaves in a few hours."

Lisa stood up and gave her friend one more hug. "Call me the second you get home."

"I will." Wendy gave a small smile. "At least one good thing happened today. I beat you in basketball."

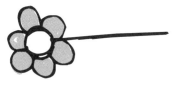

What do YOU Think?

* If you were Lisa, what would you say to Wendy?

_____

_____

_____

* Describe the last time you experienced both ups and downs in one day.

_____

_____

_____

* Have you lost a loved one or do you know a friend who has?

_____

_____

_____

·Tiny Tip· Life is unpredictable and some days are better than others. If you learn to trust God to take care of you, you will be better equipped to deal with the things you can't control.

Trust in the LORD with all your heart and lean not on your own understanding; in all your ways submit him, and he will make your paths straight.
Proverbs 3:5-6

Try It! Surviving Tough Times

As much as we'd like to experience only the good things in life, we need to be able to cope when bad things happen. Try these simple strategies when life gets tough.

What to do:

1. Walk your dog, ride your bike, or put on music and dance around the room. Exercise will lift your spirits.

2. Write a story and place the heroine in your shoes. Why not write a happy ending?

3. Do something nice for someone else. When you concentrate on others, you won't focus so much on yourself.

4. Start a gratitude journal. Add five things you are thankful for every day. Read your list often.

5. Clean your room. Having a tidy space will bring order to your life.

6. Tell a friend how much you appreciate her.

7. Think about how life will be a week, a month, or a year from now. What feels overwhelming at the moment will lessen in time.

8. Join a club, tryout for a sport, or learn a new skill.

9. Eat a healthy diet. Add more fruits and vegetables to keep your body happy.

10. Make the most of the time God has given you. Do something positive *right now* to improve your life.

Did YOU Know? By keeping your eyes on Jesus and what the Bible says, the ups and downs of life won't seem so overwhelming. God gives you promises in Scripture that will not only help you during the hard times, but also will encourage you during the good times.

You will keep in perfect peace those whose minds are steadfast, because they trust in you.

Isaiah 26:3

REAL Life 101

UPS and DOWNS = good and bad times.

Have you ever ridden a roller coaster? As the train of cars goes up the tracks, your palms grow moist and your heart races anticipating the big drop ahead. Once you go over the first peak, the roller coaster's speed increases and your body shifts this way and that as you go over the highs and lows of the track. Some roller coasters even have vertical loops that turn your body upside down!

Does your life ever feel like one big roller coaster ride?

One day you may have the best birthday party ever and the next you may wake up with the flu. One day you may make a new friend and the next your beloved pet dies. One day you may win first place, and the next you break your leg. One day you may experience sunshine and the next a storm hits.

Each day you are given situations that make you grow and teach you lessons about life. And let's face it. **Days would be pretty boring if you didn't have challenges.** The bottom line is you become a stronger person when you experience both the ups and the downs.

For Fun Ups and Downs Trick

What you need:
- Three matching plastic cups

What you do:

1. Gather your family or friends. Tell your audience, "I will get all three cups facing up in three moves while simultaneously moving two cups at a time."

2. Set up the cups quickly so that the center cup is facing up while the two outside cups are facing down. Tell the audience, "Watch carefully."

3. With swift movements, flip the cup in the middle and the cup on the right simultaneously so that the middle cup is now facing down and the cup on the right is facing up.

4. Now flip the cup on the left and the one on the right at the same time, so that the left cup is facing up and the right cup is down.

5. For the third move, flip the middle cup and the one on the right so that all three cups are now facing up.

Why this works:

This trick is all about odd and even numbers. Since the goal is to get all three cups facing up, you need to start with one (odd) cup facing up. When you let audience members try it, place two (even) cups facing up and they'll never be able to do the trick. Basically, an odd number of cups facing up, plus an even number of cups moved at a time, equals an odd number of cups facing up. And an even number of cups facing up, plus an even number of cups moved at a time, equals an even number of cups facing up.

If you never allow your audience to know to start with only one cup facing up, you'll stump them every time! **Have fun!**

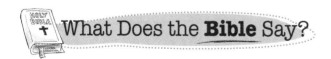
What Does the **Bible** Say?

Have you ever been so tired that you fell asleep in the car, watching TV, or while doing your homework? Sometimes life can be overwhelming. Read these Bible verses to encourage you today.

Isaiah 40:28-31

28 Do you not know?

Have you not heard?

The LORD is the everlasting God,

the Creator of the ends of the earth.

He will not grow tired or weary,

and his understanding no one can fathom.

29 He gives strength to the weary

and increases the power of the weak.

30 Even youths grow tired and weary,

and young men stumble and fall;

31 but those who hope in the LORD

will renew their strength,

They will soar on wings like eagles;

they will run and not grow weary,

they will walk and not be faint.

 Letters to **GOD.**

Dear God,

Wendy was gone for a whole week! Montana sounds like a great place to visit, but I doubt it felt like a vacation to my friend. I couldn't wait until she came over to tell me about her grandfather's funeral and what it was like to be with her aunts, uncles, and cousins she hadn't seen since second grade. (It would be fun to fly in a plane one of these days! My whole family lives close by, which is good and bad if you know what I mean.) Anyway, I couldn't wait until her mom dropped her off. Since it was Saturday, we had the whole day to do whatever we wanted.

When our doorbell rang, I jumped up from the couch thinking it was Wendy. Instead, it was the mailman with a package for my dad— more computer stuff, I bet. (Maybe he bought something for me. I can dream, right?)

While I was waiting for Mrs. Taylor to pull into our driveway, I looked at the clock at least a hundred times. When she didn't come by noon, Mom said I could call her to see why she was taking so long. After the fourth ring, Mrs. Taylor answered the phone. She said they were driving down my street when Wendy threw up in the car. BLAH! So they turned around and went home. Apparently, Wendy's cousin had the stomach flu and passed it around to the whole family. I felt bad for Wendy, but honestly, I felt worse for myself. Now what was I going to do all day? After a few minutes thinking about it, I decided to make Wendy a card instead of feeling sorry for myself, because Wendy is just not anyone. She's my best friend!

Love,
Lisa

Jot it down

Now, it's your turn. Write your own letter to God and tell about a time you chose to do something positive when life got tough.

_____

_____

_____

_____

_____

_____

_____

_____

_____

_____

_____

_____

_____

_____

_____

*Let us throw off everything that hinders and the sin
that so easily entangles. And let us run with perseverance
the race marked out for us, fixing our eyes on Jesus,
the pioneer and perfecter of faith.*

Hebrews 12:1-2

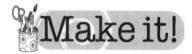 # Make it!

Dried Flower Note Cards

When was the last time you made a hand-written card for someone? It's easier to send an e-mail or text, but try making these dried flower note cards. The people you send them to will appreciate your thoughtfulness.

What You Need:

✳ Tweezers

✳ Flowers and leaves

✳ White absorbent paper towels

✳ Note cards

✳ Colored pencils

✳ White glue

✳ Toothpick

✳ Self-adhesive contact paper

✳ Construction Paper (Optional)

What To Do:

1 Pick your flowers and leaves late in the morning after the dew has dried. Choose different sized flowers. Be careful. Some flowers, like roses, have thorns!

2 Time to press. Remove all the stems from the flowers, and spread the blossoms and leaves in a single layer on a sheet of white absorbent paper. Place a second sheet of paper over it, and set a heavy book on top. Leave for about 2 weeks.

3 Now that your blooms and greenery are dried it's time to get creative! Decide how you want to arrange your flowers and leaves on a blank piece of paper. Take a pair of tweezers and pick up a leaf that you want for the background. Be gentle as your leaves and flowers can be brittle. Using a toothpick dipped in white glue, apply a small amount to the back of the leaf. Place on the note card.

4 Next, glue on all the focal, or big flowers. Glue the same way as the greenery. Once this is done, add the accent or smaller flowers. Continue this process until you are satisfied. Let dry.

5 Now that your flower arrangement is complete, write a quote, a poem, or nice message on the front or you can leave it blank for a simple, but beautiful look.

6 To protect your card, cover it with clear self-adhesive contact paper. Press contact paper down firmly to make sure it sticks to the flowers, greenery and card. For extra color, glue onto construction paper.

Here are some ideas for a message inside the card:

- Please accept my heartfelt sympathies for your loss.
- My thoughts are with you and your family during this difficult time.
- Sending you thoughts of peace and courage.
- May your heart and soul find peace and comfort.
- My thoughts and prayers are with you.
- I love and care about you.

 Memory Verse

Write down the memory verse from the beginning of the chapter. Memorize it. What are you thankful for today?

_____

_____

Takeaway Thought

You will experience good and bad times—and maybe all in the same day! When you have God by your side, there is no reason to fear. You can trust that he will take care of you.

 Prayer

Dear God, prepare me for the ups and downs of life. Help me to be strong and focus on you. In Jesus' name, Amen.

* Chapter 6 *
Making the Grade

Whatever you do, work at it with all your heart,
as working for the Lord.

Colossians 3:23

Nicole's Substitute Teacher

Nicole walked into her classroom Monday morning and noticed the giggles and whispers right away.

Tara motioned to her. "Hey, Nicole, come here quick. Before the substitute teacher walks in."

Nicole didn't like the sound of that, but walked up to her friend anyway to hear what all the laughter was about. "What's up?"

"Everyone is going to sit in different seats," Tara chuckled. "So, you're going to be me and I'm going to be you."

"Why would we do that?" Nicole shrugged a shoulder. "Won't that confuse the substitute teacher?"

"Yeah." Tara nodded. "That's what's so funny about it. Then, after lunch, we'll sit in our regular seats."

Nicole looked around the room and noticed no one was sitting where they should be. She realized she'd be the only one not going along with the prank.

"Hurry, Nicole," she heard someone say from across the room. "I think the substitute is coming."

Tara stood by her desk motioning for her to move. "Quick, here she comes."

Nicole slid out from her desk and plopped into Tara's seat located behind hers near the door. She situated herself, glanced at the girl next to her, who was

trying to keep a straight face, then looked over at the door as . . . Mrs. Clayton, her neighbor, walked in.

What should she do? Nicole had to think of something fast. Her stomach knotted.

Mrs. Clayton turned and placed her briefcase on the teacher's desk. Her back was toward Nicole. Here was her chance. She jumped up from her seat, grabbed Tara, and made a quick exit.

"What are you doing?" asked Tara. "It's just a little joke. Why so serious?"

Nicole pulled her down the hallway into the girl's bathroom. She sucked in a breath and slowly let it out. "Our substitute is my neighbor. She would know we're up to something if I sat in your seat and went by the name of Tara."

"Quick thinking." Tara looked at herself in the mirror and ran her fingers through her hair.

"We'd better hurry before she marks us tardy."

The girls went back to their classroom and sat down in their proper seats. "Nicole, so good to see you." Mrs. Clayton stood in front of the class.

Nicole's cheeks grew warm. "Nice to see you too, Mrs. Clayton." She felt a slight tug on her long hair.

"Phew, that was close," Tara whispered behind her.

Nicole wouldn't get in trouble because she was in the correct seat, but after lunch when everybody else switched, the joke would be out and poor Mrs. Clayton would be confused.

Nicole liked Mrs. Clayton. She often cared for Nicole's bird when her family was on vacation. Mrs. Clayton lived alone and was getting old, but she used to teach every day before she retired. Plus, her neighbor made the best chocolate chip cookies and would share them with her after school. Suddenly, Nicole wanted the trick to be on the kids in the class and not on Mrs. Clayton.

Nicole couldn't concentrate on the lesson and was distracted whenever Mrs. Clayton called the students by someone else's name. Finally, the recess bell rang, and everyone grabbed a snack from their backpacks and scrambled out the door. Nicole lingered by her desk.

"Nicole, it's fun to be in your class today." Mrs. Clayton pulled out a chocolate chip cookie from her lunch bag. "Would you like one, dear? I brought two."

She couldn't resist the dessert. "Thank you." As she approached her neighbor, an overwhelming feeling came over her. "Mrs. Clayton, I have to tell you something—"

"I already know that the kids are not sitting where they should be." A chuckle escaped Mrs. Clayton's lips.

Nicole's eyes grew wide. "How'd you know?"

Her neighbor pulled out the school yearbook. She flipped through the pages pointing to some of the kids in her class. "I like to look through the most recent yearbook before I substitute teach." Mrs. Clayton took a bite of her cookie. "I ask for a list of the children and look them up so that I know who's who."

"Wow," said Nicole. "And we thought we were fooling you."

"We?" asked Mrs. Clayton. "But you and Tara are sitting in the correct seats."

"We weren't when you first walked in. That's why Tara and I bolted out the door. I realized you would know our trick, and I didn't want to get caught. I'm sorry."

Mrs. Clayton chuckled. "You're forgiven. Now run along and get the sugar out of your system."

Nicole finished the last bite of her cookie, sprinted out the door, and found her friend Tara waiting for her by the oak tree.

"What took you so long?"

"Just chatting with Mrs. Clayton," said Nicole. "She's one smart lady."

"What makes you say that?"

"You'll see," said Nicole.

Once back in the classroom, Nicole couldn't wait to see the looks on the kids' faces when Mrs. Clayton called everyone by their real names with no problem. But she never called on anybody. Instead, she had everyone write their names vertically on a piece of paper, then think of words that described themselves for each letter of their name. During the art project, Mrs. Clayton walked around the room and talked with each of the students one by one, asking if she could help them think of an adjective. While everyone worked, she smiled at Nicole a few times.

After coloring, Mrs. Clayton had everyone read his or her project to the class. Nicole stood when it was her turn. "Nicole. N is for nice, I is for interesting, C is for cool, O is for original, L is for leader, and E is for excellent."

After school, Nicole saw several students go up to Mrs. Clayton and apologize for trying to trick her earlier in the day. She smiled at each one stating that she knew all along.

Walking home from the school bus, Nicole realized that God is kind of like Mrs. Clayton. He already knows everyone by name. He knows everything we say, do and think even when we try to hide it! She couldn't fool God even if she tried.

A smile curved Nicole's lips as she ran up her lawn and into her house. "Hey Mom, you're never going to guess who was our substitute teacher today!"

What do YOU Think?

✱ If you were Nicole, what would you have done when Tara asked to switch seats?

_____

_____

_____

✱ Have you ever had a substitute teacher? What was he or she like?

_____

_____

_____

✱ Why is it important to do your best in school?

_____

_____

_____

•TiNy TiP• God expects you to work to your ability. Getting all A's on your report card is not as important as doing your best. And remember to keep your eyes on your own paper.

Do your best to present yourself to God as one approved, a worker who does not need to be ashamed and who correctly handles the word of truth.

2 Timothy 2:15

Try It! Being Your Best

Learning should never be boring. Even your worst subject can be interesting if you have a good attitude. A student who works hard has a brighter future than the kids who don't. Do each of these suggestions to help you do your best in school. When you've mastered each one, place a check mark next to the number. You'll be amazed how your grades will improve.

What should you do?

1. _____ Get organized. Buy a separate folder for each subject or get a notebook with separate color-coded dividers. Make sure you only keep the papers for that subject in the proper place. Throughout the year, throw away papers you no longer need.

2. _____ Write down your assignments. You may think you have a great memory, and you probably do, but why rely on your brain when you can have everything written down in a notebook? You can also fill in other commitments, like sporting and church events so that you manage your time effectively.

3. _____ Study. One simple way to study for a quiz or test is to write down vocabulary words on one side of a 3" x 5" card, and the definitions on the other. Memorize each side and test yourself both ways.

4. _____ Participate in class. When your teacher asks a question, don't be afraid to raise your hand. Even if your answer is wrong, it shows the teacher that you want to learn and you'll remember the right answer when it comes time for the test.

5. _____ Ask questions. Instead of getting frustrated, approach your teacher to help you understand. It's better to think through the problem and gain more knowledge, than shrugging it off and hoping you'll comprehend it later.

6. _____ Join clubs or do sports. There's more to life than school. You'll learn more when you aren't studying 24/7.

7. _____ Set goals. Maybe your goal is to hand in all your assignments, or to make a certain grade on a test. Whatever you decide, stick to it. You'll see your grades improve little by little.

8. _____ Be your own advocate. Even teachers make mistakes. If you think you deserve a better grade than the one you received, talk to the teacher. He or she will see that school is important to you and may consider how to help you improve your grade.

9. _____ Extra credit. If your teacher offers extra credit, do what's required. You never know when those extra points will come in handy.

10. _____ Have fun! Yes, you can enjoy school when you put your mind to it.

Fun Facts about YOUR school.

Fill in the blanks:

✳ What is the name of your school? _____

✳ Are you home schooled? _____

✳ What grade are you in? _____

✳ What is your teacher's name? _____

✳ How many kids are in your class? _____

The *Girl's* Guide to Life.

✳ Where is your desk? _____

✳ Who do you sit by? _____

_____

✳ What is your principal's name? _____

✳ What time does your school start? _____

What time does it end? _____

✳ What is your favorite subject in school? _____

Why? _____

✳ What is your least favorite subject in school? _____

Why? _____

✳ Does your school have a library? _____ What is the name of

your favorite book? _____

✳ Does your school have a cafeteria? _____ If so, what is your

favorite meal? _____

✳ Do you like your school? _____ Why or why not? _____

_____

Did **YOU** Know? When you work with all your heart, the Bible says it is an act of worship and you bring glory to God. In other words when you do your best in school, you are working for Him and not for people.

Therefore, my dear brothers and sisters, stand firm. Let nothing move you.
Always give yourselves fully to the work of the Lord, because you know
that your labor in the Lord is not in vain.

1 Corinthians 15:58

REAL Life 101

GRADE = the mark you receive for the quality of your work.

Which describes you?
File cabinet personality

You get up every morning at the same exact time, have your clothes laid out the night before, go to school prepared, expect nothing lower than an A on your report card, do your homework the minute you get home, eat dinner, read, go to bed early.

Junk drawer personality

You get up after your mom calls you for the hundredth time, run around the house looking for a clean pair of jeans, race to the bus stop, misplace your homework, glance at your notes before a quiz, memorize your assignments, watch TV all afternoon, eat dinner, whip through your homework, go to bed late.

If you're like most students, you probably fall somewhere in between. Most kids need help getting organized, preparing for the day ahead, staying on top of their homework, and making sure they go to bed on time. To be successful in school, your parents' job is to keep you balanced. They should be involved, set limits, and encourage you to excel, but they shouldn't do your work for you.

Here are some handy tips to keep in mind:

- **Keep a routine**—get up at the same time every morning, eat a nutritious breakfast, find a time and place to study after school, and read for 20 minutes before laying your head on your pillow.

- **Plan ahead**—choose your clothes for the next day before you go to bed and put everything you need for school into your backpack, including completed homework assignments and anything else you need the following day.

- **Limit distractions**—keep your television, computer, phone, and video game usage to a minimum, especially on school nights.

- **Stay curious**—talk with your parents about what's going on in the world, visit museums, and read the newspaper to keep up on current events. Your intellect will grow.

- **Allow free time**—if you have every minute planned, it means you're too busy. In order to replenish your energy, make sure you have time during the day to unwind.

So how important are good grades anyway?

Important if you plan to go to college, but don't focus so much on the letter on top of your paper, but the quality of the work you hand in.

Did you take your time?

Do you understand the concepts?

Did you ask the teacher for help when you needed it?

Can you honestly say you did your best?

✴ If you answered "yes" to each of these questions, then you should feel good about your work and your grade will reflect that.

✴ If you answered "no" to any of the above questions, then you need to step it up and take ownership of your schoolwork. After all, it's your job!

One final tip:

Don't fall into the perfection trap. Everyone makes mistakes. Likewise, if you know you can do better, challenge yourself.

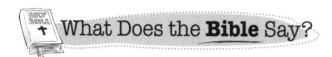 What Does the **Bible** Say?

Did you know it honors God when you do your best in school? When you work hard on every paper, test, and project, you bring glory to God. You'll be amazed at how good you'll feel. Here's what the Bible says about laziness.

Lazy hands make for poverty, but diligent hands bring wealth.

Proverbs 10:4

A sluggard's appetite is never filled, but the desires of the diligent are fully satisfied. Proverbs 13:4

For even when we were with you, we gave you this rule: "The one who is unwilling to work shall not eat." 2 Thessalonians 3:10

If anyone, then, knows the good they ought to do and doesn't do it, it is sin for them. James 4:17

No discipline seems pleasant at the time, but painful. Later on, however, it produces a harvest of righteousness and peace for those who have been trained by it. Hebrews 12:11

 Letters to **GOD.**

Dear God,

I wanted to cry when I saw the big red F on the top of my social studies test. I admit I didn't study very long and only filled out half the study guide, but I knew the test was going to be multiple choice and I'm good at guessing the correct answer, right? Wrong!

At break, Tara asked me what grade I got. I didn't want to admit that I failed, so I told her I got a C. Yep, I lied. UGH! I felt even more like a failure when she told me she aced it. I'm not surprised. Tara never gets anything lower than an A-. She'd have a heart attack if she did! I, on the other hand, am a B student when I study my brains out and am fine with that, but an F? There's no excuse. I just didn't study enough.

In my defense, the pipe burst in our bathroom the night before the test and water gushed out into the hallway and into my bedroom closet. By the time my mom turned off the main line, water had already come through the downstairs light fixture. How could I study with big fans drying out the floor and ceiling? I wish I had asked my mom to write a note to my teacher. Maybe he would've let me take the test another day. Oh well, too late now.

On the bright side, Tara and I were the last two standing for the class spelling bee today. Since I'm a better speller, Tara asked if I'd like to study with her so that we can beat everyone in the whole school. At first I said no because I wanted to be beat Tara too, but then I changed my mind. And while we're studying together maybe she can help me with social studies. I know she'd be glad to do it.

Love,
Nicole

Jot it down

Now, it's your turn. Write your own letter to God and tell him about a time you helped a friend study.

_____

_____

_____

_____

_____

_____

_____

_____

_____

_____

_____

_____

_____

*Give generously to them and do so without a grudging heart; then because of this the L*ORD *your God will bless you in all your work and in everything you put your hand to.*

Deuteronomy 15:10

Make it!

Chalkboard

By helping a friend study you also gain knowledge and God will bless you. As you make this chalkboard, think about how you can work with all your heart.

What You Need:

＊ A smooth flat sheet of wood, such as veneered birch—24" x 24" x 1/4"

＊ Primer paint

＊ Chalkboard spray paint

＊ Sandpaper

＊ Newspaper

＊ Brushes

＊ Chalk

Before you start: Ask your parents for permission and make sure you wear eye and breathing protection when you sand wood or use spray paint. Always spray aerosol cans outside in a well-ventilated area, and always have an adult supervise. All products can be purchased at a craft, hardware, or an all-purpose store. Read all of the manufacturer's directions and precautions.

What To Do:

1. Spread the newspaper out to protect your work area.

2. Sand the wood sheet, then paint with the primer. Primer seals the wood so that the chalkboard paint will stick better. Put on two coats and then sand for best results.

3. Once the primer is dry, spray the wood sheet with chalkboard spray paint according to the manufacturer's directions. Let dry and repeat with second coat. Spray one coat horizontally (side-to-side) and the other coat vertically (up and down).

4. Once it's dry, attach it to a wall and draw or write with chalk to your heart's content.

 Write down the memory verse from the beginning of the chapter. Memorize it. How can you work for the Lord with all your heart?

_____

_____

_____

Takeaway Thought

School is hard work. You need discipline and motivation to do well.

 Prayer **Dear God,** thank You for school. Help me to do my best. In Jesus' name, Amen.

Chapter 7
Standing Firm

Put on the full armor of God, so that you can take your stand against the devil's schemes.

Ephesians 6:11

Jenna's Decision

Jenna rocked to the beat of the music blaring from her speakers.

"Jenna." Mom knocked on Jenna's bedroom door and peeked her head into the room. "Are you ready to go the mall?"

"Yeah, I just need to grab my purse and find the gift card." Jenna flipped off the music and grabbed a piece of gum she spied on her dresser.

"I'll meet you in the car," said Mom. "We only have a couple of hours to shop for school clothes."

Jenna fingered through her wallet and found the brightly colored gift card her grandma sent her for her last birthday. Smiling, she put it back into her wallet and made her way to the car.

Mom started the engine and Jenna buckled her seat belt. They drove the short distance to the mall and parked in the parking lot.

"What do you need today?"

Her mom was very practical and would only buy her the necessities.

"Well," said Jenna, "my pants have holes in the knees, and I really need a new coat." She wanted a whole new wardrobe, but she thought she better stop while she was ahead.

"You've grown quite a bit. We'll see if we can find some T-shirts too."

Jenna smiled at her mom and continued walking toward the entrance. Her friend stood near the double doors. "Hey look, Mom. There's Riley and her older brother." Jenna raced forward. "Let's catch up with them." When they were within earshot, she called out, "Riley, over here."

Riley turned. "Hi Jenna!"

"Do you want to come clothes shopping with us?"

"It sure beats hanging out at the arcade. My mom's working today." Riley made arrangements to meet her brother in an hour.

"Come on, we don't have much time." Jenna linked arms with her friend and darted inside the mall.

After scouring the racks, Jenna tried on jeans, T-shirts and coats. She wished they'd shop at the expensive trendy store at the other end of the mall, but this one did have some cute clothes. Her mom kept running back and forth grabbing different sizes and styles while Riley helped put the discarded clothes on hangers. She finally decided on three pairs of jeans, a half dozen T-shirts, and a blue coat . . . all on sale!

"Mom, can we look at the earrings at *Claire's*?" Jenna asked as they stood in the cashier line.

"Sure. But stay there. I'll come after I'm done paying."

"Thanks." Jenna and Riley took off toward the jewelry store.

They had fun looking at the bracelets, necklaces and rings, pretending they could have any piece they wanted. They moved to the earrings displayed on the racks. Jenna

picked out some long, dangly ones knowing her mom would never approve. She put them back on the rack and turned to say something to Riley when she saw her friend slip a pair of earrings into her pocket. Jenna hid behind the rack of jewelry not knowing what to do. Why would Riley take the earrings without paying for them first? She knew her friend's parents gave her an allowance. It didn't make sense. What should she do? She bit her lip and took a deep breath.

"There you are," said Mom. "We'd better get Riley to the arcade before her brother comes looking for her."

Jenna panicked. "Um, Mom, wait! I haven't used my gift card yet."

"I'll help you find something after we drop Riley off." Her mom handed her one of the shopping bags. "Can you hold this one? These bags are heavy."

Jenna carried the one that held her new coat. "Actually, I've already picked out a pair of earrings." She looked directly at her friend and gave her the "I saw what you did" look. "Riley is holding them for me. Can you show my mom the earrings?"

Riley pulled the earrings out of her pocket. "Here they are."

Jenna nearly choked. The earrings were big black squares with fake pearls in the middle.

"You picked these?" Mom gave Jenna a strange look.

Jenna snatched the earrings out of Riley's hand and quickly put them back on the rack. "Oh, no, those are the wrong ones. Where are they?" She scanned the jewelry rack trying to find a pair she liked. "How about these?" Jenna held up a pair of simple silver dangly butterflies.

"That's better," said Mom. "How much are they?"

"Twelve ninety-nine," said Jenna. "With my $15 gift card, I have enough for the tax, too."

"I'll wait for you two on that bench." Mom gestured to the one just outside the store.

Jenna waited until her mom left and she was alone with Riley and whispered, "What were you thinking?"

"It's my mom's birthday in a couple of days and I forgot my money," said Riley.

"So, you were planning on taking them?" asked Jenna. "That's called shoplifting!"

"I know." Riley hung her head. "That was a dumb idea, huh?"

They ambled to the cash register line. "Will you be able to come back to the mall to buy those earrings before your mom's birthday?"

"I don't know," said Riley. "I could see if my brother has any money left."

"Or maybe I could use my gift card for your mom's earrings, and come back later for these." Jenna looked at the pretty butterfly earrings.

"No," said Riley, "that's all right. I just remembered that my mom already has a similar pair. Maybe I'll buy her some nice smelling soap or something."

"You're sure?"

"Yeah." Riley nodded. "And thanks for watching out for me. I knew it was wrong."

The person in front of Jenna finished paying.

"What are friends for?" Jenna set the butterfly earrings on the counter and dug in her wallet for the gift card.

"By the way, those are really cute earrings." Riley grinned.

"Thanks," said Jenna. "I think so too."

What do YOU Think?

✱ When was the last time you went shopping for clothes? What did you buy?

_____

_____

✱ What is the difference between wanting and needing something?

_____

_____

✱ What would you do if you saw your friend shoplifting?

_____

_____

•Tiny Tip• Temptations are everywhere, encouraging you to live a higher lifestyle than what you can afford. Ads shout at us from the Internet, magazines, television, and movies, but it comes with a cost (and not just money). Instead of thinking of others, your focus shifts to yourself. The temptation to want what the world sees as important can push you to make poor choices.

Do nothing out of selfish ambition or vain conceit.
Rather, in humility value others above yourselves.
Philippians 2:3

Try It! Wearing God's Armor

In order to be strong and stand firm when the devil tries to tempt us, we need to put on the armor of God. But what does that mean? Try this exercise to keep spiritually fit.

Scenario #1:

Victoria thumbed through a magazine and sighed when she saw the star of her favorite television show. Her clothes, hair, and make-up were perfect and it appeared so was her life. She had the cutest little white-haired dog poking out of her oversized bag and she was last photographed coming out of a well-known Hollywood restaurant. Victoria read the article and her stomach did a flip. According to the magazine, the famous actress didn't believe in God. Victoria had always looked up to the seventeen-year-old star and now suddenly didn't know what to think about her own faith.

✳ Where should Victoria look to find the answers she's searching for?

_____

_____

The Belt of Truth:

Roman soldiers wore a wide belt to hold their swords, ropes, darts, and rations sack. The belt was the first thing a soldier put on and was tied in several different places to hold it securely around his waist so that he'd have weapons at the ready. If the belt was in the incorrect position, it could cost the soldier his life.

Like the belt was to the soldier, so is the Word of God to your life. It keeps you strong and protected. By using the Bible as the belt of truth, you will have a solid foundation to fight off evil and keep life in perspective.

If you hold to my teaching, you are really my disciples. Then you will know the truth, and the truth will set you free.
John 8:31-32

Scenario #2:

Megan couldn't believe her ears when she heard Chloe tell the teacher Megan had written the curse words on the bathroom wall. Megan's fists balled and she wanted to slug Chloe, but thought better of it. Mom wouldn't be too happy if she did that. Her mom had enough troubles dealing with her older brother. How was Megan going to get out of this one? Her teacher had to know the truth.

* What would you do if you were Megan?

_____

_____

Breastplate of Righteousness:

After the soldier put on the belt, he anchored a lightweight breastplate crafted of metal bands to protect his chest and heart from powerful blows. If a soldier failed to wear his breastplate, he risked an arrow piercing an internal organ.

The devil is quite tricky and works hard to hurt you with slanderous accusations, but when you put on the breastplate of righteousness your heart will be protected. Because of what Jesus did for us by dying on the

Scenario #5:

Natalie sat among the girls in her Bible study questioning whether or not heaven was real. Her small group leader explained that if she believed that Jesus died for her sins, she would spend eternity with Him. Natalie had a hard time imagining forever. From her experience, everything on earth had a beginning and an end. She thought back to when she was six years old the night she accepted Jesus into her heart. Was that really all she had to do to go to heaven?

✳ What does Colossians 3:2 say? How would this verse help Natalie?

_____

_____

Helmet of Salvation:

Made from bronze or iron, a Roman soldier's helmet protected his skull and neck from enemy blows and falling debris. The helmet was fashioned with a chinstrap, visor, and two hinged sidepieces to cover the cheekbones and jaw. Rank was distinguished by the color of the horsehair plume attached to the top of the soldier's helmet used during ceremonies.

The biggest battle you face will be in your mind and the devil wants nothing more than for you to question your salvation. To be on guard and have a clear mind, put on the helmet of salvation by praying and reading the Bible.

Sovereign Lord, *my strong deliverer, you shield my head in the day of battle.*
Psalm 140:7

Scenario #6:

Across the field, Gabriella saw Kaylee hunched over, hugging her knees to her chest. Her best friend had received a mean text message over the weekend and didn't want to hang around anyone. Gabriella had to do something to make her feel better, but what? A Bible verse popped into her head. "For if you forgive other people when they sin against you, your heavenly Father will also forgive you." (Matthew 6:14) If she shared the Bible verse with Kaylee, maybe her friend would be able to forgive the girl that hurt her. After all, everyone sins and needs to be forgiven.

✳How does remembering a Bible verse help Gabriella?

_____

_____

Sword of the Spirit:

The soldier carried a two-edged sword that was tipped upward on the end and cut in two directions, which inflicted more damage than any other sword and made it easy to kill the enemy. By alternating between a forward thrust of the shield and plunge of the sword, a soldier could press back the enemy one step at a time.

By quoting Scripture, you are using God's Word as your sword of the Spirit. As a Christian girl, you have been given authority by God to use his words to bring others to him.

For the word of God is alive and active. Sharper than any double-edged sword, it penetrates even to dividing soul and spirit, joints and marrow; it judges the thoughts and attitudes of the heart.
Hebrews 4:12

▷ Are you fully dressed with the armor of God? By wearing the Belt of Truth, Breastplate of Righteousness, Sandals of Peace, Shield of Faith, Helmet of Salvation, and Sword of the Spirit, you will be fit for life's battles.

Did **YOU** Know?

Every day you make decisions in what you say, what you do, and how you act. The devil would like nothing better than for you to fall into his trap by gossiping, wearing inappropriate clothing, hanging out with the wrong crowd, or trying worldly things like drugs and alcohol. As a Christian girl, you've been given the Holy Spirit to empower you, as well as spiritual weapons to fight off the evil forces of this world.

Be on your guard; stand firm in the faith; be courageous; be strong.
1 Corinthians 16:13

REAL Life 101

STAND FIRM = holding on to what you believe, speaking up for what is right, and walking away when you're tempted.

To stand firm in your faith, you need to make smart choices in every area of life, including how you act and what you say, from stepping up when a friend is doing something wrong, to how you spend time on the computer. Here are some helpful hints to keep you smart and safe online.

Make a pact with your parents that you will:

- Obey the rules they set for when you can use the computer, how much time, and which sites are appropriate.
- Never share a photo of yourself or any personal information such as your address, telephone number, or where you go to school without your parents' permission.

- Never agree to meet someone in person that you connected with online unless your parents arrange the meeting and go with you.
- Keep your passwords a secret and never give them to your friends or anyone online. (Except your parents, of course!)
- Trust your gut if you feel uncomfortable or threatened because of something online. Tell your parents immediately.
- Check with your parents before you download or install software, otherwise you may give your computer a virus or jeopardize your family's privacy without realizing it.
- If you get a mean message online, don't respond. Instead, tell your parents. It's not your fault you received it in the first place.
- Have fun! Technology is amazing and learning new things online is a great way to further your knowledge about the world.

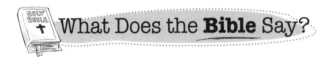 What Does the **Bible** Say?

Standing firm in your faith is difficult.
In fact, it's easier to just give in to temptation, but don't do it! Jesus shows us how to be strong in Matthew 4:1-11 when he was tempted by Satan. Read the story in your Bible and write down what Jesus says in verse 10 here:

_____

_____

_____

_____

_____

_____

 Letters to **GOD.**

Dear God,

My mouth hung open in shock and disbelief when I saw my friend Robin smoking a cigarette behind the school the other day. Robin had told me several times that she would NEVER hang around Jade. I guess she changed her mind.

I was going to sneak away when Robin and Jade saw me, and motioned me over. I had a sick feeling in the pit of my stomach, but I walked over to them anyway. I figured I could see what they wanted and still be able to catch my bus before it left.

Robin held out the cigarette and asked me if I wanted to try it. Part of me wanted to, but another part knew it was wrong . . . and disgusting! My mom has always told me that smoking is addictive and unhealthy. Plus, I've heard once you start it's hard to stop. Suddenly I was sad and scared for my friend and knew I had to stand up for what was right. So I shook my head and walked away. I heard Jade laugh and say something mean about me.

You'll never guess what happened next. Robin raced after me and told me I was the very best friend she ever had and that if I could say no to smoking, so can she! Wow, I was blown away. Robin also admitted that she'd been hanging out with Jade lately and that she'd been encouraging her to do things Robin knew were wrong (like shoplifting!). When we found our seat on the bus, Robin smiled at me and said she was glad she had a Christian friend like me. Thanks, God! You're awesome.

Love,
Jenna

Jot it down

Now, it's your turn. Write your own letter to God and tell Him about a time you let your light shine for Him by being a good example to one of your friends.

_____

_____

_____

_____

_____

_____

_____

_____

_____

_____

_____

_____

In the same way, let your light shine before others,
that they may see your good deeds and
glorify your Father in heaven.

Matthew 5:16

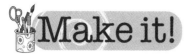

Make it!

Sand Candleholder

When you stand firm, you draw others to God. As you make this sand candleholder, think about how you can shine your light for him.

What You Need:

* Glass jar
* Sand (or rice)
* Small round candle
* Food coloring
* Ribbon
* Glue

What You Do:

1. Place the sand (or rice) in a glass or metal bowl and use the food coloring to tint the sand the desired color.

2. Fill the jar about two thirds full with the colored sand (or rice).

3. Put a candle into the middle of the jar, pushing it into the sand.

4. Glue and/or tie a ribbon around the jar.

Write down the memory verse from the beginning of the chapter. Memorize it. How can you be on guard, courageous, and strong so that you stand firm in your faith?

_____

_____

By putting on the armor of God, we can fight off the devil's schemes.

 **Dear God,** thank you for your Word. Help me to hold on to what I believe, speak up for what is right, and walk away when I'm tempted. In Jesus' name, Amen.

Chapter 8
Bodies in Motion

Do you not know that your bodies are temples of the Holy Spirit,
who is in you, whom you have received from God?
You are not your own; you were bought at a price.
Therefore honor God with your bodies.

1 Corinthians 6:19-20

Samantha's New Attitude

Samantha touched the ground first with her left hand and then with her right as her legs swung overhead. She stood and lifted her hands high in the air in a gymnast's pose.

Bethany clapped. "Nice cartwheel. Are you practicing for the meet this Saturday?"

"Yeah," said Samantha. "I'm waiting for mom to take me to the gym."

Bethany hopped on her bike, her books under one arm. "See you later. I'm going to study at Carrie's house."

Samantha watched her sister ride down the street. Sometimes, she wished 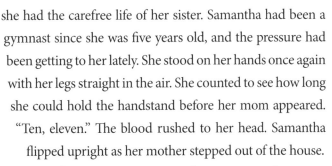 she had the carefree life of her sister. Samantha had been a gymnast since she was five years old, and the pressure had been getting to her lately. She stood on her hands once again with her legs straight in the air. She counted to see how long she could hold the handstand before her mom appeared.

"Ten, eleven." The blood rushed to her head. Samantha flipped upright as her mother stepped out of the house.

"Time to go to practice." Mom swung her purse over her left shoulder, the car keys jingling in her hand. "Where's your duffle bag?"

Samantha pointed to the bag sitting by the back tire.

Mom opened the trunk and placed it inside. "Ready to go?"

"Ready as I'll ever be." Samantha sighed before climbing in. She buckled her seat belt.

Mom started the car's engine and backed out of the driveway. "What's going on? You feel okay?"

"I'm fine." Samantha shrugged a shoulder. "Guess I'm just a little nervous about Saturday."

"Samantha, I've seen all of your routines, and they're great. I really believe you're ready—"

"I guess . . ."

"Butterflies aren't necessarily a bad thing," said Mom. "They keep you on your toes."

Samantha stared out the window. She'd never been afraid to do front handsprings, back flips, and balance moves until recently, and during practice she constantly told herself she was going to fall down or mess up. She even started having nightmares. Should she tell her mom about her negative thoughts?

"It's all in my head," Samantha said instead as they drove down the freeway.

"You're right. Most of gymnastics is what goes through your mind," said Mom. "You can have all the talent in the world, but if you don't believe you can do it, then you probably won't."

As they rounded the last turn before reaching the gym, Samantha took a deep breath and whispered a little prayer. *"Dear Lord, help me clear my mind."*

Mom pulled into a parking spot. "Do you want me to stay or can I run a few errands while you practice?"

"You can go." Samantha got out of the car and grabbed her bag from the trunk.

"I'll be back in a couple of hours. Remember, you're amazing, not only in gymnastics, but also your sweet spirit. You can do it." Mom waved and drove away.

"Hey, Samantha. You coming in or not?" asked Tiffany, her fiercest competition. "It won't matter if you practice. I'm going to win on Saturday, no matter what."

"Of course I'm coming in. I can't be beat that easily." Samantha opened the door and walked in first.

I can do it. I believe I can. I can do it. I believe I can, Samantha repeated to herself. She dropped her duffel bag in the corner of the gym and joined the group of eight girls sitting in a circle on the floor.

"Today we're going through practice like it's the competition," said Coach Pamela. "This is our last one before the meet, so I want to see entire routines at each apparatus."

Samantha peeked at Tiffany and quickly turned around when their eyes met. She was more determined than ever to do her best.

"Remember to focus and think positively." Coach Pamela walked around the circle. "You've practiced your routines plenty of times to feel confident. The assistants will spot while I float around to see how you're doing. Let's start."

Samantha was glad she was paired with Brooke. It would be easier for her to concentrate if she didn't have Tiffany breathing down her neck. As Brooke did her floor routine, Samantha thought about how easy it was to slip into her old pattern of negative thinking. *"Not this time. I know I can do it."* She clapped for her teammate as Brooke left the mat.

Samantha took a big breath as she walked onto the floor to do her routine. Out of the corner of her eye, she could see Coach Pamela standing next to the assistant for the floor exercise. *"I can do it,"* she repeated to herself one more time. She struck a pose and waited for the music to begin.

With each tumbling pass, Samantha's confidence grew. She moved with precision and grace, mixing dance moves with leaps and twists. For her final move, Samantha did a front walkover into the splits, then raised her hands high as the music came to an abrupt stop.

"Way to go, Samantha," called Brooke.

Samantha stood, a smile tugging at the corners of her mouth.

"Very nice, Samantha." Coach Pamela gave her a big hug. "That's what I like to see. Do that again on Saturday, okay?"

Samantha nodded. "Thank you, Coach."

"I need to get over to the balance beam. Tiffany is having problems. Hey, Samantha can you come with me and encourage her? You seem to have your head on straight today."

What do I say? Please fall down at the meet on Saturday? Or, it's okay if you mess up the whole day? Samantha sucked in a breath.

Coach Pamela led Samantha over to the other side of the gym. "I know it would mean a great deal to her. She looks up to you, you know."

Samantha's eyes widened. "She does?"

Samantha watched Tiffany finish her routine. Her landing was sloppy and she took a huge step to the side. Tiffany walked off the mat in a huff.

Samantha approached.

"You don't need to gloat." Tiffany turned away.

"Samantha's not gloating," Coach Pamela said. "She's here to tell you something."

"Um, you know, um," stammered Samantha. She had to think of something quick. "You're really good, Tiffany," she finally said. "You just need to clear the clutter in your brain and think positive."

Tiffany sighed. "Maybe you're right, thanks. You're not so bad yourself."

Samantha smiled, then walked away to rejoin Brooke. She still wanted to beat Tiffany, but win or lose she'd give it her all.

What do YOU Think?

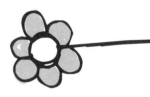

✳ Why was Samantha starting to have nightmares about messing up?

_____

_____

_____

_____

✳ Do you think winning is the most important thing?

_____

_____

_____

_____

✷ Why do you think exercise is important?

_____

_____

_____

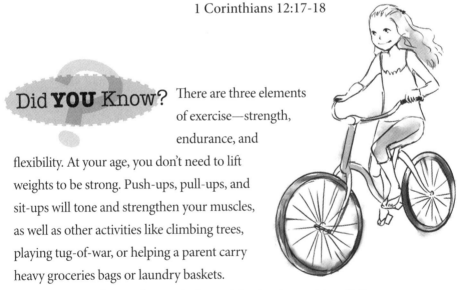

Tiny Tip According to the American Academy of Pediatrics, "Kids should be physically active for at least 60 minutes every day." For example, you can join a team and play soccer, basketball, or volleyball, or you can do an individual sport like running, swimming, or dance. The main thing is to get your body moving!

If the whole body were an eye, where would the sense of hearing be? If the whole body were an ear, where would the sense of smell be? But in fact God has placed the parts in the body, every one of them, just as he wanted them to be.

1 Corinthians 12:17-18

Did YOU Know? There are three elements of exercise—strength, endurance, and flexibility. At your age, you don't need to lift weights to be strong. Push-ups, pull-ups, and sit-ups will tone and strengthen your muscles, as well as other activities like climbing trees, playing tug-of-war, or helping a parent carry heavy groceries bags or laundry baskets. You can gain endurance by regularly participating in aerobic activity, which strengthens the heart and helps the body deliver oxygen to all its cells. Physical activity that makes the heart beat faster and makes you breath harder is aerobic exercise. Stretching at the end of your workout improves flexibility. It allows the muscles and joints to bend and move so you'll have full range of motion. By incorporating strength, aerobic, and stretching exercises into your daily routine, you'll stay lean and limber.

She sets about her work vigorously; her arms are strong for her tasks.
Proverbs 31:17

Try It! How Fit Are YOU?

Have you ever done a fitness test in P.E. class? By doing certain exercises, your teacher can measure how fit you are. But why wait till then? With the help of a parent or friend, you can get started right now.

Try these exercises:

▷ A push-up measures arm and abdominal strength as well as endurance. With your hands firmly planted on the floor, press yourself up. Make sure your shoulders are directly above your hands, your arms are fully extended with your body straight, and the toes of your shoes are curled under to hold you up. Lower yourself down to the floor without touching it, then press yourself up again. If you find this is too difficult, you may drop down to your knees to do a modified push-up. How many push-ups can you do in 30 seconds? _____

▷ The sit-up test measures abdominal strength and endurance. Lie down with your knees bent and feet flat on the floor. Have your parent or friend secure your feet while you place your hands behind your head with your elbows out. Now curl up to a seated position. How many sit-ups can you do in 60 seconds?

_____

□□□□□▷ The flexed-arm hang measures upper body strength and endurance. Grab an overhead bar with arms bent and chin slightly above the level of the bar. Try to hold this position as long as possible. If your chin touches the bar or you dip your head back, you are finished. How long can you hold a flexed-arm hang?

_____

□□□□□▷ The standing long jump measures leg strength. With your feet slightly apart, stand behind a marked line (could be the edge of a rug if doing this exercise indoors) and have a friend or parent stretch out a tape measure to measure the distance jumped. Bend your knees and swing your arms back and forth. Now jump as far as possible making sure you take off and land on both feet without falling backward. Take the best jump out of three. The measurement is taken from the back of the heel that is closest to the take-off line. How far can you do the standing long jump?

_____

□□□□□▷ The sit and reach test measures flexibility of your lower back and hamstring muscles. Sit on the floor with your legs stretched out straight ahead and your feet slightly apart against the

bottom of a step. With your palms facing downwards, reach forward as far as possible. After a few practice reaches, reach out and hold the position while your friend or parent measures how far you can reach past your feet. How far can you sit and reach? _____

 The one-mile walk/run measures heart and lung endurance. Wear comfortable clothes and sturdy running shoes. Each lap of a track represents a quarter of a mile, so four times around equals one mile. You may walk or run, but the goal is to go as fast as you can. Have a friend bring a stopwatch to measure your time. How fast can you walk or run a mile? _____

In a few months, take the fitness test again to see if you can beat your scores.

Fun Facts about Life.

* Ancient Egyptians played a game similar to bowling, with large stones set up as pins and small stones for a ball.

* Soccer is the most popular sport in the world, and the World Cup is the biggest and most important soccer competition. Soccer first appeared in the Olympic games in 1908.

* The five interlocking Olympic rings represent the five participating continents: Africa, America, Asia, Australia, and Europe. The rings first appeared on the Olympic flag in 1913.

* NFL footballs are made of cowhide leather, but smaller footballs are made from rubber. Ask your P.E. teacher which kind of football you use.

* Walter Frederick invented the Frisbee in 1957. The toy saucer was named after a pie restaurant in Bridgeport, Connecticut, because kids liked to throw the tins around after they ate William Frisbie's pies.

* Pedro Flores made the first modern yo-yo in 1928 based on a game he remembered as a child, but similar types of toys have been around for hundreds of years.

* In 1586, the first woman golfer was the queen of Scotland, Mary Stuart. Now, more than 28 million Americans play golf.

* In 1963, baseball pitcher Gaylord Perry said, "They'll put a man on the moon before I hit a home run." On July 20, 1969, a few hours after Neil Armstrong set foot on the moon, Gaylord Perry hit his first and only home run.

* Yellow tennis balls were used at Wimbledon for the first time in 1986. The first women to play in the Wimbledon tournament wore full-length dresses.

* The leotard is the gymnast's uniform and is named after French acrobat Jules Leotard. Gymnasts use chalk to improve their grip, absorb sweat, and keep blisters from forming.

REAL Life 101

EXERCISE = moving the body by doing physical activity to develop or maintain fitness.

Some girls would rather read a book, paint a picture, or study for a test than exercise. What these girls don't realize is that being active is important to looking and feeling better. Your heart is a muscle and works hard at pumping blood throughout your body. By regularly doing aerobic exercise and giving your heart a workout, your body will be in good shape and your heart will do a better job.

There are many more reasons why exercising is important. Exercise can help you:

- Have strong muscles and bones.
- Keep your body limber, and improve balance and posture.
- Lessen your chance of developing diseases like type 2 diabetes, cancer, high blood pressure, and heart disease.
- Control body fat and maintain a healthy weight.
- Lift your mood.
- Sleep better.
- Cope throughout the day.
- Improve your grades.

What Does the **Bible** Say?

Physical fitness is important to stay healthy,

but your relationship with God is more important. 1 Timothy 4:8 says, "For physical training is of some value, but godliness has value for all things, holding promise for both the present life and the life to come."

How do you become godly? Colossians 3:12-14 says,

"Therefore, as God's chosen people, holy and dearly loved, clothe yourselves with compassion, kindness, humility, gentleness and patience. Bear with each other and forgive one another if any of you has a grievance against someone. Forgive as the Lord forgave you. And over all these virtues put on love, which binds them all together in perfect unity."

 Letters to **GOD.**

Dear God,

I didn't win first place. Can you believe Tiffany and I ended up cheering for each other? We figured we'd rather have one of us win than someone we don't know. In the end, I got second and Tiffany was third. She was a good sport about it until her parents walked up. Seems as though first place is all that matters to them. Now I know why Tiffany messes up sometimes. They put pressure on her to be perfect. How awful!

Before we left the gym, Mom asked me if I wanted to stop by the frozen yogurt shop to celebrate what a good job I'd done. She also said that it looked like I was having fun and that was all that mattered. Gotta love my mom! Suddenly, I thought about Tiffany and asked if she could come with us. My mom looked shocked. Downright amazed! Guess she never thought I'd want to hang out with my biggest rival. Honestly, I surprised even myself, but after what I'd just witnessed I knew Tiffany needed some encouragement . . . and some frozen yogurt. (And there's nothing like Yogurt Palace. You can serve yourself and add as many toppings as you like. YUM!)

Guess what? Tiffany's parents didn't seem to mind. In fact, my mom invited them to come along too. At first I was scared, but I figured if my positive attitude could rub off on Tiffany, maybe my mom could help Tiffany's parents too. I was right. We had a great time! And now Tiffany and I are friends.

Love,
Samantha

Jot it down

Now, it's your turn. Write your own letter to God and tell Him about a time you encouraged a friend to stay positive.

_____

_____

_____

_____

_____

_____

_____

_____

_____

_____

_____

_____

_____

_____

Finally, brothers and sisters, whatever is true, whatever is noble, whatever is right, whatever is pure, whatever is lovely, whatever is admirable—if anything is excellent or praiseworthy—think about such things.

Philippians 4:8

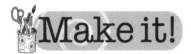

Make it!

Sock Wristband

Ready to get sweaty? As you make this sock wristband, think of what type of exercise you'd like to do in order to honor God with your body.

What You Need:

* Cuffed sock
* Scissors
* Needle and thread

What You Do:

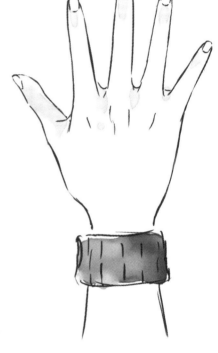

1. Cut off the bottom of the sock where it isn't stretchy. Set aside.

2. Fold the stretchy part of the sock inside out. Turn over the cut edge about a ½ inch to make a hem.

3. With a needle and thread, sew all around the edge. (Hint: Make sure you knot the end of the thread so that your hem will stay secure.)

4. Turn the wristband right side out and slip it on your wrist.

5. Put away your supplies and go for a run! Wipe away the sweat with your new sock wristband.

Write down the memory verse from the beginning of the chapter. Memorize it. What does honoring God with your body mean to you?

_____

_____

_____

Exercise is good for your mind and body and is good for overall health.

Dear God, thank you for my body. Help me to exercise every day. In Jesus' name, Amen.

Chapter 9
What's in the Pantry?

Give us today our daily bread.

Matthew 6:11

Lauren's Choice

The temperature had sky rocketed the last few days. Summer was right around the corner, but the heat had come early. Lauren ran the back of her hand across her forehead and kept walking. She thought about the chocolate ice cream her mom bought a few days ago. The walk from the bus stop never seemed so long.

Lauren stopped under the shade of an oak tree. She unzipped her backpack, grabbed her water bottle, and took a long swig. It felt good to

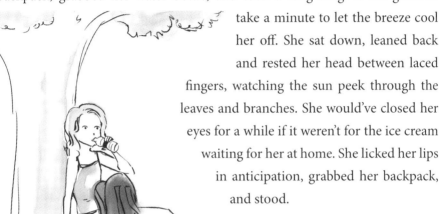

take a minute to let the breeze cool her off. She sat down, leaned back and rested her head between laced fingers, watching the sun peek through the leaves and branches. She would've closed her eyes for a while if it weren't for the ice cream waiting for her at home. She licked her lips in anticipation, grabbed her backpack, and stood.

A black cat zipped past, then Mr. Murphy's dog. Lauren didn't think anything of it until Anna, a girl a couple of years younger than she, ran past. "Help me catch him!"

"Catch who? The cat or the dog?" Lauren ditched her backpack and followed Anna.

"Jack," Anna called over her shoulder. "Mr. Murphy's on vacation and I'm dog sitting. If he runs away . . ." She let the rest of her words dangle.

Lauren knew exactly what Anna meant. Mr. Murphy loved that dog. He bought the little terrier when his wife died several years back. Lauren was glad she wasn't Anna right now, but she could help.

"We'll catch him together," Lauren said. The girls ran down the street in pursuit of the runaway dog.

"I think I saw him go in there." Anna pointed to the open gate that led into Dylan's yard.

135

"I'll wait here," said Lauren. There was no way she'd go near Dylan's house. Every once in a while the boy smelled like garlic and he never talked to any of the girls. Ever.

"But I need your help," pleaded Anna. "See him there." She pointed toward the vegetable garden where Jack was digging a hole. The dog must have found a bone.

A shiver ran up and down Lauren's spine. Maybe Dylan buried something—or someone out there.

"If I go this way and you go that way, we might have a chance to grab him." Anna made a circular motion with her hands. The girl was smart, Lauren had to give her that, but to chance it and go into Dylan's yard? The worried look on Anna's face made Lauren change her mind. Maybe Dylan wouldn't see them.

With each step, the girls closed in on Jack. Lauren raised her fingers one at a time and mouthed, "One, two—"

"Who's out there?" a voice bellowed before she got to three.

Jack stopped digging and darted across the yard. He ran through the open gate and took off running.

"No!" Anna balled her fists and let out a frustrated moan.

Dylan stood a few feet away from way from them. "What are you doing in my yard?"

Why should they both have to spend more time with Dylan than they had to? Lauren motioned for Anna to stay on the dog's trail. "I'll explain, then catch up to you."

Anna nodded and took off after Jack.

The sun beat down on Lauren's head. Beads of sweat trickled down her neck. She wished she had her water bottle, but she'd left her backpack under the oak tree. Maybe she should let Anna find Jack on her own and go home. The ice cream would taste good about now, but first she had to explain to Dylan before he asked any more questions.

"Anna's taking care of Mr. Murphy's dog and he escaped from his yard."

"That was Mr. Murphy's dog?" Dylan asked as he straightened his posture. "I'll help you catch him."

Since when did he talk to girls?

"Really? You don't have to." Lauren held up a hand. "I'm sure Anna's already caught him by now." She took a few steps backward and bumped into something hard.

"Watch out," Dylan called.

Lauren glanced over her shoulder. A dirt-stained wheelbarrow sat on its side. "Thanks."

Dylan motioned for Lauren to follow him. "Let's catch up to Anna and see if she's found Jack." He smiled, revealing a straight row of white teeth. He was kind of cute.

Oh boy! That thought didn't just cross my mind.

They ran back the way she and Anna had come. The oak tree came into view. Lauren snatched her pack.

When they reached Mr. Murphy's house, Lauren spotted Anna sitting on the front porch with Jack in her lap. "How'd you get him back?"

"I didn't." Anna smiled. "He ran home and snuck through the hole he dug under the fence."

Dylan grabbed the shovel leaning against Mr. Murphy's shed. "Here, let me fill it."

"Now I know why he keeps it handy." Anna wagged her head and glared at the dog. "You scared me."

"Don't be too mad at him. At least he came home," said Lauren. "Time for me to go home too. I've got cookies-and-cream ice cream waiting for me."

"Mmm," said Anna. "Sounds good."

Dylan patted the pile of dirt with the shovel. "Yeah, must be nice to have ice cream on such a hot day."

"Okay, I get it." Lauren rolled her eyes. "You two can come home with me. But not a word of this at school."

"You wouldn't want everyone to know you invited garlic boy over." Dylan smirked.

"Well, um—"

"I've heard the rumors." Dylan said. "I guess it serves me right. But if you'd ever tasted my mom's lasagna, you'd eat it for breakfast too."

Lauren grinned. She had had leftover pizza for breakfast, but lasagna? Never. She pressed her lips together to keep from laughing.

"I haven't had ice cream in months." Anna set Jack down and opened the door. The dog scampered inside. "My mom said she's having a hard time paying the bills and there's no room in the budget for treats—like ice cream."

Wow! Lauren had no idea. How could she live so close to Anna and Dylan and know so little about them? "I'm sorry to hear that," said Lauren. "I have two older brothers and my mom has to keep the refrigerator and pantry stocked. Hey Dylan, if you don't mind me asking, what do you keep buried in your yard?"

"I'll never tell." He wagged his head.

Garlic boy was definitely cute . . . and very mysterious. Lauren always liked a good mystery.

Her stomach rumbled. Tonight before bed she'd pray for Anna and her family. She'd also thank God that her family always had food—especially ice cream.

What do YOU Think?

✽ What is your favorite food?

_____

_____

_____

✱ What was Lauren most concerned about in the beginning? Did it change as the story unfolded?

_____

_____

_____

✱ How can you put aside your feelings to help someone in need?

_____

_____

_____

 •TiNy Tip• We all like special treats like ice cream and cake, but if we ate it all the time we'd consume too much fat and sugar. In order to be healthy, we need to eat a variety of foods including fruits, vegetables, whole grain, and protein found in dairy products such as cheese, eggs, milk, and yogurt, as well as beans, fish, nuts, and meat.

Everything that lives and moves about will be food for you.
Just as I gave you the green plants, I now give you everything.
Genesis 9:3

Food Facts Quiz:

Take this quiz to see how much you know about food. Circle the answer you think is correct.

1. After you go grocery shopping with your mom or dad, how long do you have before you need to put the food in the refrigerator?

      30 minutes   2 hours

      4 hours   24 hours

2. How many eggs does a chicken lay in one year?

    75   130   280   320

3. What is inside the corn kernel that makes it pop when heated?

    Oil   Sodium

    Sugars   Water

4. Tomatoes are rich in which vitamins?

    B6 and B12   D and E

    A and C   K and P

5. What is the most popular apple variety in the United States?

    Red Delicious   Gala   Granny Smith

6. Eating a large amount of carrots will turn your skin orange.

    True   False

7. Which part of a potato contains the most nutrients?

    The skin   The inside   They are the same

8. How are green bell peppers and red bell peppers related?

    Green and red peppers aren't related

    Green peppers are immature red peppers

9. Guacamole is . . .

    A freshly prepared condiment made from chopped tomato, onion, and chili peppers

    A dip made from mashed avocados, onions, and lime juice and is often served with tortilla chips

    A creamy beverage made from pulverized rice and milk and seasoned with cinnamon, sugar, and vanilla

10. Which Asian culture rarely eats with chopsticks?

Japanese   Chinese

Thai   Korean

11. What is the most traditional bean used to make chili?

Garbanzo bean   Black bean   Pinto bean

12. American bacon comes from what part of the pig?

Hindquarters   Loin   Belly

13. When was the ice cream sundae invented?

1960s   1770s

1890s   1920s

14. Swallowing chewing gum takes seven years to completely digest.

True   False

15. Kids who don't always have enough food at home perform just as well as kids who get enough daily nutrition.

True   False

Correct Answers:

1. 2 hours. But if the temperature outside is above 90 degrees, certain food items such as meat, poultry, and milk should be put in the refrigerator within 1 hour.

2. Chickens lay around 280 eggs each year, but they traditionally lay more eggs in the spring and summer when the days are longer and brighter.

3. Water. When a corn kernel is heated, the water that exists inside the kernel becomes steam and expands, eventually breaking the hard outer covering of the kernel and turning it inside out. The soft starch of the interior becomes fluffy and white after the tiny explosion, creating popcorn.

4. A and C. Vitamin A aids in the growth of skin and bones, and vitamin C helps the body produce collagen in bones, cartilage, muscle, and blood vessels, as well as aids in the absorption of iron.

141

5. Red Delicious. There are 100 varieties of apples grown commercially in the United States. Red Delicious is the most popular, followed by Gala, Golden Delicious, Granny Smith, and Fuji.

6. True. The same pigment that gives carrots their bright orange color can also cause your skin to develop an orange tinge. Once your body has absorbed all the beta-carotene it can handle, the excess gets stored in superficial connective tissue, which can make you look orange.

7. Skin. The skin and the layer just below contain extra fiber and many nutrients. Next time your mom makes mashed potatoes, ask her to leave the skin on.

8. Green peppers are immature red peppers. The variety of pepper plant and the stage of ripeness determine the color and flavor of bell peppers. Green bell peppers are simply unripe red or yellow peppers.

9. Guacamole is a dip made from mashed avocados, onions, and lime juice and is often served with tortilla chips. It can also include chopped tomatoes, garlic, and jalapenos.

10. Thai. The Chinese started using chopsticks during the Shang Dynasty, between 1600 and 100 BC. The Japanese, Korean, and Vietnamese cultures have also been using chopsticks for a very long time.

11. Pinto bean. Arguments have raged for decades over what bean to use in chili. Pinto Beans are the typical classic, but many people enjoy black beans or kidney beans, too.

12. Belly. American bacon is a cut of pork that comes from the belly of a pig. High fat content is necessary to achieve a sweet flavor and the desired crispness once the bacon is cooked.

13. 1890s. The ice cream soda was invented in 1874, but some people complained that the beverage was too sinfully rich to eat on Sundays. So ice cream merchants removed the soda water from the equation, creating the ice cream sundae.

14. False. Once you swallow a piece of gum, it loses its sticky quality and is just another morsel of food to your digestive track. Don't worry, the gum won't linger in your stomach.

15. False. Kids who lack proper nutrition and are from low-income homes are more likely to experience irritability, fatigue, and difficulty concentrating, making it hard to perform at school.

Fun Facts about Life.

∗ What time do you typically eat breakfast? _____

Lunch? _____ Dinner? _____

∗ What is your favorite cereal? _____

∗ What else do you like to eat for breakfast? _____

_____

∗ If you make a sandwich, what do you put on it? _____

_____

∗ What do you like to drink? _____

∗ When you get home from school, what snack do you grab? _____

_____

∗ What's your favorite fruit? _____

Vegetable? _____

∗ You're at the grocery store with a friend and have a few dollars in your

pocket. What do you buy? _____

_____

∗ What do you like to eat for dinner? _____

_____

∗ It's your birthday and you can choose any dessert you want. What do

you choose? _____

✳ You can't sleep and your stomach is rumbling. Do you wait for

breakfast or go to the kitchen and grab a snack? _____

Eating habits have changed over the years . . .

• A typical breakfast in the 1900s might include creamed toast and fruit, prairie chicken stewed, fried potatoes, and sliced tomatoes.

• During the 1920s, pineapple upside-down cake and Jell-O molds became popular as well as tea sandwiches and fancy salads.

• A simple dinner of the 1950s might be pigs in blankets, baked tomatoes with cheese, banana sherbet, and butterscotch brownies, along with soda pop in the bottle (if you could get it) or Tang, a drink made from orange crystals and sugar—and used as a beverage for astronauts on space missions.

• Some popular soups of the 1970s include beef barley, chicken corn chowder, cream of asparagus, or meatball soup.

• Americans turned to comfort food such as mac'n' cheese, pizza, and chicken potpie after our country suffered one of its worst disasters in 2001.

• Beginning in 2009, families began packing more brown-bag lunches and preparing home-cooked meals because of the tough economy.

Did **YOU** Know?

When you go through the teenage years you'll have a bigger appetite. You'll grow taller, your body will develop curves, and your weight will increase. Now is the time to make wise food choices. God made your body and wants you to take care of it.

Taste and see that the LORD is good; blessed is the one
who takes refuge in him.

Psalm 34:8

REAL Life 101 ◁·····

FOOD = contains essential nutrients, such as carbohydrates, fats, proteins, vitamins or minerals, and is consumed to give you energy, maintain life, and stimulate growth.

Share these tips with your parents and friends on how to build a well-balanced meal:

1. Make half your plate fruit and vegetables.

2. Add meat, such as beef, chicken, or pork. Don't forget seafood at least twice a week.

3. Include bread, pasta, or rice made from whole grains.

4. Remember to add a dairy product such as a glass of milk or low-fat yogurt.

5. If you need something on your veggies for taste, try a sprinkle of Parmesan cheese or some low-fat dressing.

6. Chew your food slowly. There's no need to rush.

7. Try new foods. You never know, you may discover a new favorite.

8. Eat sweets in moderation. Try a healthy dessert like a fruit bar.

9. It's fun to go out to restaurants, but home-cooked meals are better for you and cost less.

10. Sit down at the dinner table with your family as often as possible. There's no better time to share what's happening in your life than mealtime.

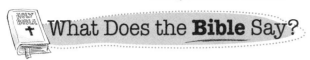

What Does the **Bible** Say?

Did you know fruit is mentioned in the Bible?

This kind of fruit can change your life. Look up Galatians 5:22-23 and unscramble the words to discover the hidden message. *Answers appear at the back of the book.*

VOLE   ___ ___ ___ ___
                     10

YOJ   ___ ___ ___
        6

PAECE   ___ ___ ___ ___ ___
      12

CIENAPTE   ___ ___ ___ ___ ___ ___ ___ ___
          8   4

NIDSSNEK   ___ ___ ___ ___ ___ ___ ___
       14

SODGOSNE   ___ ___ ___ ___ ___ ___ ___ ___
                   11

SANTIFLEHSUF   ___ ___ ___ ___ ___ ___ ___ ___ ___ ___ ___ ___
       1   13 15 9 7 3

SNTENEGSEL   ___ ___ ___ ___ ___ ___ ___ ___ ___ ___
          5

FELS-LORTONC   ___ ___ ___ ___ - ___ ___ ___ ___ ___ ___
                                2

___ ___ ___ ___ ___   ___ ___
1   2   3   4   5   6   7

___ ___ ___   ___ ___ ___ ___ ___
8   9   10   11   12   13   2   14   15

 Letters to **GOD.**

Dear God,

I had a great time with Anna and Dylan this afternoon. We had fruit smoothies. At first I was mad my brothers had eaten all the ice cream, but the berry smoothies were D-E-L-I-C-I-O-U-S! We cooled down in no time.

Chris, my oldest brother, kept giving me the eye. I guess he remembered all the times I talked about Dylan—and not necessarily in a good way. I pulled Chris aside and told him how Dylan helped Anna and me hunt for Mr. Murphy's dog, Jack.

Mr. Murphy is like a grandpa. In fact he's one of the nicest men I know. The day my family moved in he brought over an apple pie and ice cream. It was good! And last week he came over with fresh strawberries. He knows how to make us feel special. I wonder if he brings treats to Anna's house. From what Anna told me today, it sounds like they could use the extra food.

After we finished our smoothies, Anna left to check on Jack. It was kind of awkward having Dylan over by himself. Josh, my other brother, asked Dylan if he wanted to hang out and play basketball. I thought it was nice of Josh to ask even though Dylan said he had to go home. I guess he hangs out with his grandma (she has Alzheimer's Disease and can't be left alone for very long) until his mom comes home from work. Besides being grateful for food, I'm also thankful that my grandparents are healthy.

Love,
Lauren

Jot it down

Now, it's your turn. Write your own letter to God and tell Him what you're thankful for.

_____

_____

_____

_____

_____

_____

_____

_____

_____

_____

_____

_____

_____

_____

*Give thanks to the L*ORD*, for he is good;*
his love endures forever.

Psalm 107:1

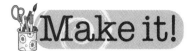

Make it!

Healthy Snacks

Eating your fruits and vegetables is important to staying healthy, and adding them to snacks is a perfect way to make sure you're getting your daily allowance. As you make these snack recipes, thank God for food.

Homemade trail mix

In a bowl, mix your favorite nuts (cashews, unsalted peanuts, almonds, walnuts, or sunflower seeds) with dried fruit (apples, pineapple, cherries, or raisins). Add some whole-grain cereal if you like.

Smoothie:

Blend low-fat yogurt with frozen fruit. You could even make a smoothie by blending milk, fresh or canned fruit, and ice. There's really no wrong combination. Yum!

Pizza:

Use a whole-wheat English muffin, bagel, or pita bread to use as the crust. Top it with tomato sauce, low-fat cheese, and cut up vegetables such as green peppers, tomatoes, onions, and mushrooms. Put in a 350-degree oven for five to ten minutes. Delicious!

Write down the memory verse from the beginning of the chapter. Memorize it. What healthy food choices have you made today?

_____

_____

 **Takeaway Thought**

Healthy food helps our body grow and develop and gives us energy.

 Prayer <u>**Dear God,**</u> Thank you for food. Help me give to others in need. In Jesus' name, Amen.

Chapter 10
Green Stuff

*Keep your lives free from the love of money and be content
with what you have, because God has said, "Never will I leave you;
never will I forsake you."*

Hebrews 13:5

Paige's Money

Paige turned her bank over and watched the dollar bills and loose change spill onto her bed. Separating the quarters, dimes, nickels and pennies as well as the one-dollar bills from the fives, Paige smiled in delight. She didn't realize she had accumulated so much over the past several months since her birthday. Paige counted her money, making sure she wrote down the exact amount before running downstairs to tell her mom how much she had.

Paige walked into the kitchen. "Mom, where are you?"

"In the laundry room. What's up?"

"You'll never believe how much money I have."

"I give up." Mom shoved clothes into the washer. "How much money do you have?"

"Grandma and Grandpa gave me 20 dollars for my birthday, so it's more than twenty."

"And…" Mom poured the liquid laundry detergent into the washer, "I just gave you your allowance for last month, so it's more than twenty-five."

"It's more than thirty because I earned five dollars from the neighbor for  picking up their mail while they were gone on vacation." Paige grinned. She leaned against the wall of the laundry room with her arms folded across her chest.

"So, my guess would be forty dollars."

"I have fifty-three dollars!" said Paige. "Can you believe it? I'm rich. I can't wait to go to the mall and spend it."

"Hold on there, my dear." Mom picked up the laundry basket and placed it on top of the washer.

Mom said "my dear." That can only mean one thing.

"Am I in trouble?"

"No. I want you to think about what you want to do with your money before you go out and spend it."

Paige followed her mom into the kitchen. "Okay, I'll think about it. But can you believe I have fifty-three dollars?"

Mom smiled and gave Paige a squeeze.

The telephone rang.

"We'll talk more later," said Mom.

Paige nodded, then ran back upstairs, sat down on her beanbag chair, and looked at her money spread across her bed in neat piles. She pulled out a piece of paper from her backpack along with a pen and started writing down the things she wanted to buy.

Jewelry, make-up, art supplies, and maybe a new T-shirt or two. Paige grinned at her list. She didn't really need anything, but buying new stuff would be fun. She couldn't wait to show her mom her carefully thought-out plan. Footsteps coming down the hall caught her attention. Quickly before her nosy little sister came into her room, Paige collected her money and put it back in her piggy bank. Before she could finish, a knock sounded on her door.

"Paige, I need to talk with you." Mom's voice sounded gentle.

"Come on in. I want to show you something, too."

Her mom walked in and sat on her bed. "Okay, you go first."

Paige handed her mom the piece of paper. "Can you take me to the mall now?"

"Wow, some list." Mom kept her eyes on the paper. "Maybe we can go this weekend."

"Great!" Paige jumped up from her bed, swung her arms in the air in a victory dance.

"Come. Sit back down. I need to tell you something."

Paige knew by the look on her mom's face that it was something serious. She joined her mom on the bed. "What's up?"

"Mrs. Johnson called, Madison's mom—"

"Madison hasn't been in school lately," Paige interrupted.

"Your friend is in the hospital. They just found out she has diabetes."

Paige's throat constricted. "Is she going to die?"

"No," said Mom. "She has been quite sick, though. Her parents are learning what she can and can't eat along with how to give her insulin injections to keep her well."

"When will she be back in school?"

"Hopefully next week."

"I'm going to make her a card."

"I'm sure she'd love that." Mom stood up to leave.

"Can we go to the hospital and visit her?"

"Sure. I'll call Madison's mom and ask if tomorrow would be a good day."

Paige went to her desk and pulled out some construction paper along with markers, glue and scissors. As she made her friend a "Get Well" card, thoughts of her shopping list popped into her mind. She remembered her dad talking about tithing and how important it was to give back ten percent to the Lord. He had said, "It's all really God's money anyway." Paige pulled out five dollars and thirty cents from her bank and put it in an envelope. She wrote "God's money" on it to bring to church. That left her with forty-seven dollars and seventy cents.

She knew she didn't want to spend all her money at once. Her dad also told her about the importance of saving. Paige decided to keep five dollars in her bank. That left her with forty-two dollars and seventy cents. She heard her mom calling.

Paige got up from her desk and sat at the top of the stairs. "Yeah, Mom."

"Mrs. Johnson said that Madison is going home tomorrow, but we can visit her in the hospital tonight if you'd like."

A new idea formed in Paige's mind. "Do we have time to go to the mall and buy Madison a present and a "Get Well" balloon? I've decided to use some of my money to cheer her up."

"I'm proud of you. We'll go right after dinner."

"Thanks. I'd better hurry and finish my card."

What do YOU Think?

* Do you know that God wants you to be happy with what he's given you? How does that make you feel?

_____

_____

_____

* If you had fifty-three dollars, what would you do with it?

_____

_____

_____

* How was Paige a generous friend?

_____

_____

_____

·Tiny Tip·   Tithing is a way of saying thanks to God for all the blessings He has given you. He wants you to give with a grateful heart, however, and not because you feel like you should. The easiest way to remember to tithe is to set money aside when you first receive it.

Each of you should give what you have decided in your heart to give, not reluctantly or under compulsion, for God loves a cheerful giver.
2 Corinthians 9:7

155

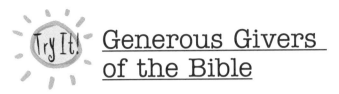

Generous Givers of the Bible

There are many people in the Bible who gave generously. Look up the Bible verses and fill in their names to complete this puzzle. *Answers appear at the back of the book.*

Down

1. Melchizedek blessed him, and he gave Melchizedek a tenth of everything. ~ Genesis 14:18-20
2. He was a centurion and gave generously to those in need. ~ Acts 10:1-2
3. He made a vow to God that he would give a tenth of all he had. ~ Genesis 28:20-22
8. This tax collector offered to give half of his possessions to the poor and would pay back four times the amount if he had cheated anybody out of anything. ~ Luke 19:8

Across

1. He brought an offering—fat portions from some of the firstborn of his flock. ~ Genesis 4:4

4. He sold a field he owned and brought the money and put it at the apostles' feet. ~ Acts 4:36-37

5. They opened their treasures and presented Jesus with gifts. ~ Matthew 2:11

6. She gave all she had. ~ Luke 21:1-4

7. He contributed from his own possessions for the burnt offerings. ~ 2 Chronicles 31:2-3

9. Though he was rich, yet for your sake he became poor. ~ 2 Corinthians 8:9

Fun Facts about Life.

✻ The Massachusetts Bay Colony was the first to issue paper money in the American colonies in 1690.

✻ The reason why U.S. currency (dollar bills) is green is because it was readily available when they were first being printed and now it's a color that people identify with having strong and stable credit.

✻ Most coins have a copper filling with another metal on the outside, usually a mix of copper and nickel.

✻ In 1943, pennies were made of zinc-coated steel to conserve copper for the war, giving them a silvery look.

✻ "In God We Trust" was first printed on coins during the Civil War, and was on all coins by 1955.

✻ Abraham Lincoln was the first person whose image appeared on a regular U.S. coin in 1909.

✻ Queen Isabella of Spain was the first woman whose image appeared on a U.S. commemorative coin in 1893.

✱ In 1926, Calvin Coolidge became the first living president whose image appeared on a U.S. coin.

✱ If you stacked a million $1 bills, the pile would be around 361 feet high.

✱ If you take a trip to Japan, make sure to exchange your dollar bills for yen. In France, you'd exchange your bills to euros. And in Mexico, you'd use pesos instead of dollars.

Did **YOU** Know? The amount of money you have does not determine your worth. God loves you whether you have a penny or a million dollars. In the Bible it says that God promises to provide for all your needs. He knows what's best for you. Do you trust Him?

And my God will meet all your needs according to the riches
of his glory in Christ Jesus."
Philippians 4:19

REAL Life 101

MONEY = coins and bills that are used to pay for things such as food, clothing, and shelter.

There is a difference between *needs* and *wants*. A need might be more shampoo, new clothing or bedding when they get worn out, or a new backpack for school. Typically, your parents buy these for you but some kids receive an allowance and use it to purchase things they need. A *want* may be a movie ticket and popcorn when you're out with friends. Shopping is fun and buying something new feels good. But the feeling doesn't last for long and the next thing you know it, you want to buy something else. The best way to learn to be content with what you have is by not comparing your life to others.

$$$ – Sit down with your parents and ask them questions regarding money. Have a family meeting to talk about the types of bills your parents pay, such as for the house, food, water, electricity, and family vacations. Ask if you could open up a savings account if you haven't already.

$$$ – What can you do to earn money? Have a lemonade stand, a bake sale, or babysit. Walk the neighbor's dog on a regular basis or make handmade jewelry to sell. Be creative! It's fun to be your own boss.

$$$ – What's credit? Let's say you want to buy something that costs more than the amount you have. If you put the purchase on a *credit card*, the bank pays the store for you and then bills you for that amount the following month. At the time, you can pay the bank the full cost of the item or make small monthly payments until the balance is paid off. Monthly payments may be convenient, but you'll pay more in the long run because of the interest the credit card companies charge for the use of a credit card. Instead, save, save, save! You'll be glad you did.

Remember, the most expensive items are not necessarily the best. Shop around. Who knows, you may find exactly what you're looking for in a discount store. Why spend more money than you have to? And here's a little hint: You can't buy happiness.

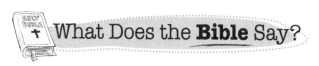

What Does the **Bible** Say?

In Mark 12:41-44, Jesus sat inside the temple watching people drop their money into the collection box. Many rich people put in large amounts of money. Then a poor widow placed two pennies in the collection box. Jesus called his disciples together and said, "I assure you, this poor widow has given more than all the others. They gave a small part of their wealth, but she, poor as she is, has given everything she has."

What does this mean for you? By putting in all she had, the widow showed God that she trusted Him with her future. Jesus loves you and wants you to rely on Him for all your needs—including food, clothes, and shelter.

Match up: Look up these Bible verses and draw a line that completes the verse. *Answers appear at the back of the book.*

Matthew 6:31-32

So do not worry, saying, 'What shall we eat?' or 'What shall we drink?' or 'What shall we wear?'

Don't be afraid; you are worth more than many sparrows.

Matthew 7:11

If you, then, though you are evil, know how to give good gifts to your children,

according to the riches of his glory in Christ Jesus.

Luke 12:7

Indeed, the very hairs of your head are all numbered.

how much more will your Father in heaven give good gifts to those who ask him!

John 21:6

He said, "Throw your net on the right side of the boat and you will find some."

For the pagans run after all these things, and your heavenly Father knows that you need them.

Philippians 4:19

And my God will meet all your needs

When they did, they were unable to haul the net in because of the large number of fish.

 Letters to **GOD.**

Dear God,

Hospitals give me the creeps. I kept hearing funny beeping noises, and then a nurse came into the room and took Madison's temperature, pulse, and blood pressure. I would hate to get poked and prodded, but Madison didn't seem to mind. After a whole week, I guess she's used to being in the hospital. Madison showed me how the bed worked and what button to press if she needs help. Most of all, she shared what it was like finding out she has diabetes.

By the way, Madison LOVED the balloon and stuffed animal I gave her. For a minute I wished I had saved my money when I saw all the flowers, cards, and presents in her room. But then I remembered that verse about it being better to give than to receive and knew I'd done the right thing. Plus, I knew Madison was happy by the way she hugged the stuffed dog and tucked it next to her in bed.

On the way home, Mom and I stopped at the grocery store to buy milk and a few other things. I got to pick out a box of cereal and now I can't wait for breakfast! When it was time to pay, Mom used her debit card. She told me it was like writing a check and that the money comes straight out of her checking account. I never paid attention to how quickly the bill adds up. Groceries aren't cheap.

After seeing how cute Madison's stuffed dog was I decided to start saving my money for a REAL puppy. I don't know which kind I'll get or if Mom and Dad will actually let me get one. They'd say it was definitely a want and NOT a need! Think I'll ask them tomorrow.

Love,
Paige

Jot it down

Now, it's your turn. Write your own letter to God and tell Him about a time you were responsible with your money and saved for something big.

_____

_____

_____

_____

_____

_____

_____

_____

_____

_____

_____

_____

_____

His master replied, "Well done, good and faithful servant!
You have been faithful with a few things; I will put
you in charge of many things.
Come and share your master's happiness!"

Matthew 25:21-22

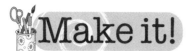

Chip Can Bank

A good place to put your dollar bills and coins is in a chip can bank. Think about how you can tithe, save, and spend your money wisely.

What You Need:

* Empty potato chip can
* Wrapping paper
* Ribbon
* Craft glue
* Scissors

What You Do:

1. Rinse out the can and wipe dry.

2. Cut a slit into the lid long enough for a quarter to fit through.

3. Cut the wrapping paper to fit around the outside of the can.

4. Glue the wrapping paper to the can.

5. Cut two strips of ribbon.

6. Glue one strip of ribbon around the top of the can, and glue the other strip around the bottom.

7. Get creative and decorate any way you'd like.

8. Put money in it.

 Write down the memory verse from the beginning of the chapter. Memorize it. How can you learn to be satisfied with what you have?

_____

_____

You need money to live, but God is the one who provides.

 **Dear God,** thank you for providing for me. Help me to be content with what I have. In Jesus' name, Amen.

Chapter 11
Dynamic Devos

Love the Lord your God with all your heart and with all your soul and with all your mind and with all your strength.

Mark 12:30

Brianna's Discovery

Brianna pulled the sleeping bag up under her chin. She enjoyed having a sleepover at her friend's house, but sometimes it was difficult to get to sleep. A soft glow illuminated from under her friend Emily's covers. "What'cha reading?"

"Oh, sorry. I thought you were asleep." Emily turned off her flashlight and the room darkened.

"No, not yet," said Brianna. "But I don't mind. I'll just turn over. Remember I share a room with my sister."

"No, that's okay. I don't want to remind you of Taylor. You've told me she stays up reading and how much it bugs you. It must be tough not to have your own room."

Brianna sighed. "Yeah. So what's it like to have a room of your own?"

"It gets lonely sometimes, but for the most part I really like having my own space. I get to decorate it the way I like and put things where I want. Oh, and if I make a mess, it doesn't bother me. Of course I'm the one who has to clean it up . . ."

As Brianna listened to her friend, her eyelids closed. She rolled onto her side and took a few deep breaths. Before long, she drifted off to sleep.

When she woke the sun was filtering through the window and it was morning.

Emily tossed a pillow and it landed on Brianna's stomach. "I thought you were going to sleep forever."

"Hey, I was tired." She threw it back and hit Emily in the shoulder. The girls laughed.

"You fell asleep while I was talking."

Brianna gave her a sheepish grin. "Sorry."

Emily shrugged a shoulder. "No big deal. When you didn't say anything, I turned my flashlight on again."

Brianna sat up and stretched. "So what were you reading—"

"Pancakes," Emily's dad called from the other side of the door. "Come and get 'em."

"Dad promised me he'd make bacon too." Emily grinned. "Come on!"

Brianna slithered out of her sleeping bag and followed Emily downstairs. Twice now her friend had avoided her question. Maybe she was writing in a journal, or reading a scary novel. Brianna sat next to Emily by the counter while her dad dished up the breakfast.

Emily bowed her head and closed her eyes. Was she praying? Brianna's family prayed before meals, but Brianna had never done it on her own before. A few seconds later, Emily's eyes opened and she poured syrup over her pancakes. "Want some? It's the best. Dad puts a little butter in it before he heats it up."

On cue Brianna's stomach growled. "That sounds good, thanks."

"Here, have some bacon." Emily's dad smiled.

Brianna grabbed two slices. They were crispy, just how she liked them.

"What are you two going to do today?"

"I don't know." Emily picked up her glass of juice and took a swig. "Stay in our pajamas, watch a movie, paint our nails."

Brianna nodded. She liked the way her friend thought.

"Sounds like a fun, lazy Saturday," said Dad.

Once the girls finished eating, they walked into the family room and looked through the instant Web movies.

"How about that one?" Brianna pointed to an action movie.

"Hmm." Emily's brows furrowed.

Brianna looked at the rating. Her parents wouldn't want her to watch the movie, but they weren't here and she could make a decision on her own. "What do you want to watch?"

Emily scrolled through the movies. "Have you seen this one?"

Brianna had seen it several times. It was funny, but kind of babyish. She nodded. "Like when I was seven." She couldn't help it if she sounded annoyed.

"Maybe watching a movie wasn't such a great idea." Emily stood. "Come on. Let's go to my room and paint our nails."

Once back in Emily's room, Brianna looked through her friend's nail polish collection. Pink, red, light lavender. *Where was the black? Dark blue? Deep purple?* "Do you have anything else?"

Emily snatched the bottle of pink from the shelf. "Nope. What you see is what you get."

Brianna chose the red nail polish. She sat cross-legged on her sleeping bag, opened the bottle, and started painting. Curiosity about what Emily was reading last night once again crept into her mind. "So what is the big secret?"

"What are you talking about?" Emily stuck tissue between her toes and started painting.

"The book. The one you hid under your covers."

Emily laughed. "It's not a secret. I was reading my Bible. I do it every night before I go to bed."

The thought never occurred to Brianna. Her parents read the Bible to her after dinner sometimes, but to do it on her own? "Oh." Brianna kept on painting. *What else was there to say?*

Emily continued. "My parents bought me a Bible for girls our age. It has all kinds of fun stuff to do and think about, and the stories are easy to understand. I'll show you once our nails dry."

"Okay." Brianna never knew there were different types of Bibles. Half the time she zoned out when her parents read from their Bible because she didn't understand most of what they were saying. "Do you pray before bed too?"

"Yeah, don't you?"

"No." Brianna finished painting her fingernails, and started on her toes. "I mean, I've said *'Help me, God'* in my head before a test at school, but besides that . . ."

"When you start reading the Bible, you'll probably pray more too. You won't be able to help yourself." Emily put the lid on her nail polish. "Talking to God will become natural, like any relationship."

A relationship? Now that was a new concept.

Emily continued. "And then you'll start making better choices—"

"Like what movies to watch and stuff like that?" asked Brianna.

"Exactly." Emily blew on her nails, then dug under her pillow and pulled out her Bible. She handed it to Brianna.

She thumbed through the pages once her nails were dry. There were quizzes and questions mixed throughout. She'd like to have a Bible like this. More importantly, she'd like the kind of relationship Emily had with God. "You know, my birthday is coming up."

Emily smiled. "Just act surprised. Okay?"

Brianna hugged the book to her chest and grinned.

What do YOU Think?

✳ Do you relate to Emily or Brianna in this story?

_____

_____

_____

✳ Do you own a Bible? If so, what's your favorite verse? If not, can you think of someone you can ask to buy you one?

_____

_____

_____

✳ Do you think reading the Bible is interesting? Why or why not?

_____

_____

_____

·Tiny Tip· If you don't know where to start reading in your Bible, open it up to the first book and begin with Genesis. You'll discover how God created the world. Or, flip to the New Testament to the book of John and read about the life of Jesus Christ.

In the beginning was the Word, and the Word was with God, and the Word was God. He was with God in the beginning.
John 1:1-2

Try It! # Bible Word Search

There are 39 books in the Old Testament and 27 books in the New Testament. Circle the books of the Old Testament hidden in the word search below. The books are listed on page 171. Not all the books of the Old Testament are included in the following word search. *Answers appear at the back of the book.*

Books of the Old Testament Word Search

S	G	O	J	P	L	T	A	I	C	S	J	P	A	Z
B	N	E	H	O	E	E	H	O	S	E	A	M	E	E
R	U	Y	N	S	S	C	V	E	G	T	O	C	S	P
E	M	J	T	E	A	H	H	I	E	S	H	N	J	H
V	B	H	O	L	S	A	U	Z	T	A	O	M	U	A
O	E	N	A	N	I	I	E	A	R	I	L	K	D	N
R	R	M	H	M	A	K	S	I	T	S	C	M	G	I
P	S	T	E	G	I	H	A	A	J	E	J	U	E	A
A	U	R	G	E	H	H	T	S	O	L	M	H	S	H
R	E	A	L	A	W	N	U	B	E	C	R	A	M	E
J	H	A	I	M	E	H	E	N	L	C	F	N	P	B
B	K	A	I	M	Y	H	A	I	D	E	B	O	J	O
H	S	C	A	D	E	U	T	E	R	O	N	O	M	Y
I	A	L	H	A	B	A	K	K	U	K	E	Z	R	A
H	T	W	T	E	X	O	D	U	S	M	L	A	S	P

AMOS	DEUTERONOMY	ECCLESIASTES
ESTHER	EXODUS	EZEKIEL
EZRA	GENESIS	HABAKKUK
HAGGAI	HOSEA	ISAIAH
JEREMIAH	JOB	JOEL
JONAH	JOSHUA	JUDGES
LAMENTATIONS	LEVITICUS	MALACHI
MICAH	NAHUM	NEHEMIAH
NUMBERS	OBEDIAH	PROVERBS
PSALMS	RUTH	ZECHARIAH
ZEPHANIAH		

Fun Facts about Life.

* The word *Bible* comes from the Greek word *biblia,* which means "books."

* Moses wrote the first five books of the Bible, known as the Pentateuch.

* "In the beginning" are the first three words in the Bible and "Amen" is the last word.

* The shortest verse in the Bible is "Jesus wept" in John 11:35.

* The word "God" appears 3,358 times in the Bible, but Song of Solomon and Esther don't mention God at all.

* Psalm 117 is the shortest chapter in the Bible with only two verses. Psalm 118 is the center of the Bible, and Psalm 119 is the longest chapter with 176 verses.

* There are 1,260 promises in the Bible.

* The phrase "do not be afraid" appears 365 times in the Bible, one for each day of the year.

✳ It would take you about 70 hours to read through the entire Bible.

✳ The Bible, whole or in part, is available in more than 1,200 different languages and dialects, and is the most popular book ever sold.

Did **YOU** Know? Do you love pizza, your cell phone, your new pair of jeans? People think about the things they care about. Do you love God with your whole heart, soul, mind and strength? If you said yes, you'll want to spend time with Him in prayer and read the Bible. Besides getting to know Him better, God's Word teaches you right from wrong.

All Scripture is God-breathed and is useful for teaching, rebuking, correcting and training in righteousness, so that the servant of God may be thoroughly equipped for every good work.

2 Timothy 3:16-17

REAL Life 101

BIBLE = God's divine and inspired words to His children. You don't always need to carry a Bible with you to remember what God says in His Word. If you memorize verses from the Bible, you'll be able to bring them to mind when you need them.

▷ Tips on how to memorize Scripture:

- Pray and ask God to help you.

- Read the verse over and over again.

- Think about what the Bible verse means.

- Create a picture from the passage in your mind or draw it on paper.

- Pick out a few words that stand out to you and memorize them first.

- To begin, memorize shorter passages.

- It's okay if you look at the verse if you get stuck.

- Practice at the same time every day.

- Sing the verse.

- Find a friend and memorize the verse together.

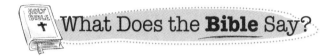 What Does the **Bible** Say?

Here are some key verses to memorize if you are:

Afraid: *Be strong and courageous. Do not be afraid; do not be discouraged, for the* Lord *your God will be with you wherever you go.* Joshua 1:9

Angry: *A gentle answer turns away wrath, but a harsh word stirs up anger.* Proverbs 15:1

Anxious: *Do not be anxious about anything, but in every situation, by prayer and petition, with thanksgiving, present your requests to God. And the peace of God, which transcends all understanding, will guard your hearts and your minds in Christ Jesus.* Philippians 4:6-7

Frustrated: *Do not let your hearts be troubled. You believe in God; believe also in me.* John 14:1

Happy: *Rejoice in the Lord always. I will say it again: Rejoice!* Philippians 4:4

Jealous: *A heart at peace gives life to the body, but envy rots the bones.* Proverbs 14:30

Lonely: *Let us love one another, for love comes from God. Everyone who loves has been born of God and knows God.* 1 John 4:7

Nervous: *I can do all this through him who gives me strength.* Philippians 4:13

Sad: *Blessed are those who mourn, for they will be comforted.* Matthew 5:4

Tired: *Come to me, all you who are weary and burdened, and I will give you rest. Take my yoke upon you and learn from me, for I am gentle and humble in heart, and you will find rest for your souls. For my yoke is easy and my burden is light.* Matthew 11:28-30

Unsure: *So we fix our eyes not on what is seen, but on what is unseen, since what is seen is temporary but what is unseen is eternal.* 2 Corinthians 4:18

Upset: *Cast all your anxiety on him because he cares for you.* 1 Peter 5:7

Worried: *Trust in the LORD with all your heart and lean not on your own understanding; in all your ways submit to him and he will make your paths straight.* Proverbs 3:5-6

⊯⊯⊯⊳ **Life is like a maze.** Without the Bible (God's Word) to guide you—you'd have a difficult time making decisions and navigating your way through. When you have a relationship with God, he helps make your path straight. (Proverbs 4:11)

 Letters to **GOD.**

Dear God,

Emily showed up at my house today and handed me a present. I guess she didn't want to wait until my birthday. My mom gave us both a funny look. Well, I ripped open the package and it was . . . a Bible! I smiled real big, hoping I looked surprised. I hugged her tight and thanked her for the gift. Emily giggled.

I can't wait to read my new Bible before bed. I might even hide under the covers and turn on my flashlight like Emily did the night I slept over. I wonder if Taylor will ask me what I'm reading.

You know what, God? I discovered it's pretty easy to talk with You. Emily told me I can write prayers to You (like I'm doing right now) or I can say them out loud or in my head. I decided writing them down works best for me. That way I can look back and see how my prayers were answered. Emily says sometimes she doesn't say anything and waits for You to whisper something to her. I wanted to try it out myself. So the other day when I was at the beach I sat quietly and waited for You to tell me a secret. And guess what? I saw creation in a whole new way. I was reminded that You made the water, fish, seashells, and everything! So cool.

I dug my toes into the sand and lifted my chin to let the sun warm me. And now besides having a few more freckles, I have a whole new appreciation for nature.

> Love,
> Brianna

Jot it down

Now, it's your turn. Write your own letter to God and tell Him about a time you saw creation in a whole new way.

_____

_____

_____

_____

_____

_____

_____

_____

_____

_____

_____

_____

_____

_____

The heavens declare the glory of God;
the skies proclaim the work of his hands.

Psalm 19:1

Make it!

Jumbo Paperclip Bookmark

As you make this craft project, think about how much God loves you and how he desires for you to spend time with him in his Word.

What You Need:

* Jumbo paper clip
* Cardboard
* Markers
* Stickers
* Beads
* Tacky glue
* Scissors

What You Do: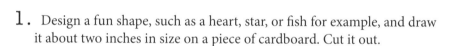

1. Design a fun shape, such as a heart, star, or fish for example, and draw it about two inches in size on a piece of cardboard. Cut it out.

2. Using your shape as a guide, draw another one on the cardboard and cut it out.

3. Color the shapes with your markers, making sure both sides are colored when you put them together. Glue beads or put stickers on your shapes, if you'd like.

4. Set the end of a jumbo paper clip on the backside of one of the shapes.   Glue it in place. Put the other shape on top and press to secure. Let dry.

5. Use it as a bookmark inside your Bible.

 Write down the memory verse from the beginning of the chapter. Memorize it. How can you show God that you love Him with your whole heart, soul, mind, and strength?

_____

_____

Takeaway Thought

When you spend time reading the Bible your faith will grow.

 Prayer **Dear God,** thank you for the Bible. Help me to read it every day. In Jesus' name, Amen.

Chapter 12
Finding Your Calling

*But seek first his kingdom and his righteousness,
and all these things will be given to you as well.*

Matthew 6:33

Morgan's Idea

Morgan and Lily raced up the ladder that led to the attic. Morgan reached the top and pushed the door open, then rushed to the chest and unlatched the lock. She smiled at all the dresses inside.

"If you're the bride, then what am I?" asked Lily, Morgan's best friend.

"You're the bridesmaid." Morgan dug into the chest and grabbed a dress in Lily's favorite color, and handed it to her.

Lily pulled the pink taffeta gown over her head.

Morgan continued to dig through the mound trying to locate the white satin dress.

"Zip me up, please." Lily turned her back. "Where did your mom get all these anyway?"

"She has four sisters and was a bridesmaid in all their weddings. Plus,  she was in a few of her college friends' weddings too."

"Cool." Lily stood in front of the floor-length mirror, admiring herself in the pink gown.

"Where could that dress be?" Morgan continued to look in other boxes scattered around the attic. She ripped the packaging tape from a box marked "Fabric" and opened it. "Hey, Lily, look what I found. Maybe we can design our own clothes." Morgan draped a bright blue piece of fabric around her neck.

"We can open up our own shop and name it *The Lily and Morgan Clothing Store*." Lily grabbed a pink floral piece and wrapped it around her shoulders.

"You mean, *The Morgan and Lily Clothing Store*." Morgan grabbed a denim piece of fabric and held it up to her waist like a skirt.

Lily shook her head. "Maybe we should just call our store *Cool Clothes* and leave it at that." She grabbed a silver metallic swatch and wound it around her head.

Morgan laughed. "Go look at yourself in the mirror. You look hilarious."

Lily walked over to the mirror, and burst into giggles. "I don't know if we'd be good designers. Maybe we should think of something else to do with the fabric." She folded the metallic piece and placed it in the box.

"We should ask my mom why she has all this fabric up here. I wonder if she's going to do something with it." Morgan neatly tucked the rest of the swatches back in the box.

"Are you going to look for the wedding dress?" asked Lily. "Otherwise, I'm getting out of this gown. I feel silly and it smells musty, like its been locked away for a long time."

Morgan laughed and helped her friend out of the pink dress. "It has been in there awhile. I wasn't born yet when my Aunt Stacy got married."

Both girls looked at each other and made a face. "Creepy!"

"Let's go downstairs for a snack and ask my mom what she's going to do with all that fabric," said Morgan.

Ten minutes later, Mom walked into the room.

Lily gave Morgan the eye and nudged her under the table.

Should I ask Mom about the fabric now? Might as well jump right in and ask. "Lily and I were up in the attic today and discovered a bunch of material inside a box. We were wondering what you're going to do with it."

Mom sat beside them. "The box has been up in the attic for a long time. I was going to make a quilt, but never got around to it. Why?"

"Oh, I don't know," said Morgan. "Just thought it would be fun to make something."

"Well if you think of something, let me know. The box has been sitting in the attic for years."

The doorbell rang.

"I wonder who that could be." Mom moved to the front door and opened it. Aunt Stacy stood in the doorway in her nurse's uniform.

"Hi, Stacy! What a surprise. Come on in." Mom waved her sister in and closed the door behind her.

Aunt Stacy dropped onto the brown leather sofa. "What a day!"

"A rough one, huh? I don't know how you work at the hospital with all those sick little kids. You've got a hard job," said Mom. "Would you like something hot to drink? Tea? Coffee?"

"Tea sounds great. I knew I came to the right place." Aunt Stacy took off her shoes and hoisted her legs onto the couch. "Hi Morgan. Hi Lily."

"Hi, Aunt Stacy."

"Hi." Lily bit into an apple slice and licked the peanut butter off her lip.

An idea started to form in Morgan's mind. "We'll be right back." She pulled

her friend by the arm into the hallway. "Come with me."

An hour later, Morgan and Lily walked into the kitchen with their hands behind their backs. "We figured out what we want to make with the fabric." Morgan smiled as she looked from her mom to her aunt, and then back at Lily. "We want to help the kids at the hospital." Morgan held up a small pillow. "We want to give them each one of these to cheer them up."

Aunt Stacy smiled. "You girls are so thoughtful. I know the children would love those pillows. Did you make them?"

"Yes," said Morgan. "I told Lily my idea, but neither one of us knows how to sew. Lily showed me how to make them without sewing. You just cut small strips all the way around two square pieces of fabric and then tie the strips together. It's easy." Morgan held up the pillow demonstrating how they made it. "We didn't know what we were going to use to fill it, but then we found some stuffing in another box. What do you think, Mom?" Morgan handed her mom the pillow.

"I think it's a wonderful idea." Mom hugged the pillow to her chest. "How many are you going to make?"

Morgan smiled. "As many as we can."

What do YOU Think?

* Who do you like to pretend to be? A bride? A nurse? A movie star?

_____

_____

_____

* If you found a box of fabric, what would you do with it?

_____

_____

_____

* How did Morgan and Lily seek God's kingdom by making the pillows?

_____

_____

_____

Tiny Tip God made you special. There is no one else like you on this entire planet. No one looks exactly like you (unless you have an identical twin, and even then there are differences) nor do you have the same personality as anybody else. You are one of a kind and God designed you for a purpose.

I praise you because I am fearfully and wonderfully made;
your works are wonderful, I know that full well.

Psalm 139:14

Personality Quiz

Every day you make choices based on your
personality. Try this quiz to discover how
God wired you.

A. You walk to the bus stop and discover the bus came early. What
do you do?

   1. Run home and find someone to drive you. The most important
thing is getting there before the bell rings.

   2. Walk to school. No big deal. Maybe I'll see a friend on the way.

   3. Go home and go back to bed. It doesn't matter if I'm a little late.
I can make a grand entrance when I finally show up to class.

B. You're doing a group project in art class.
Which task will you perform?

   1. I'll come up with the idea.

   2. I'll draw and paint.

   3. I'll present the art project to the class.

C. What is your favorite subject in school?

   1. Science or Math

   2. Art or English

   3. Choir or Drama

D. School's out! It's the first day of summer vacation. What do you do?

   1. I spend the day outside, taking pictures of flowers
and being one with nature.

   2. I make a photo collage of all my friends.

   3. I watch movies all day.

E. If you could be a certain food, which would you be?

   1. A salad.

   2. A fruit smoothie.

   3. A hamburger.

Mostly 1's: School is important to you. You enjoy discovering things and finding solutions to problems. You might consider becoming a scientist, doctor, police detective, or journalist.

Mostly 2's: You're best suited for a job that involves people. You like to have fun and your friends are at the top of your list. You might like to be a social worker, artist, writer, or teacher.

Mostly 3's: You've probably been told more than once that you're a drama queen and enjoy being the center of attention. Consider becoming a singer, dancer, actress, or any profession that puts you in the spotlight.

Each one of you should use whatever gift you have received to serve others, as faithful stewards of God's grace in its various forms."

1 Peter 4:10

Fun Facts about YOUR gifts and talents.

* Name a few things you love to do. _____

* What do people, such as your parents or teacher, tell you you're good at? If you can't think of anything, ask the people who know you best.

_____

* What comes easy to you? _____

* What is difficult for you? _____

* What do you dream of doing when you're grown up? _____

_____

_____

✱ What types of projects get you excited? _____

_____ What kinds do you dread?

_____

✱ What fills your thoughts when you lie down to go to bed? _____

_____

✱ Name a person who has made a big impact on you. _____

_____

✱ Why did you choose this person? _____

_____

✱ What do you do well that benefits others? _____

_____

Did **YOU** Know? It's easy to think only about yourself. Like most girls your age, your life is probably busy with home work, sports, church activities, family and friends. But here's a little secret. It's not all about you. Are you surprised? Look around. When you take your eyes off yourself, you discover people that need your help and see the world in a different way

Value others above yourselves, not looking to your own interests
but each of you to the interests of the others.
Philippians 2:3-4

 Letters to **GOD.**

Dear God,

The kids at the hospital LOVED the pillows Lily and I made! It was fun watching them choose which one they wanted. Some kids picked right away, while others took a few minutes to decide. Once all the kids had one, I chose a pillow for myself. The material is super soft and it's kind of a greenish blue color. It matches my comforter and looks good on top of my bed.

Seeing all those sick kids really got me thinking. What if Lily and I collected money to buy them toys? The next day, Lily and I made a plan. We'd find out what each child wanted and write it down on a wish list. Hopefully we'll collect enough money to buy them exactly what they want. Cool, huh? I never knew helping others could be so much fun.

And you know what? Since I started thinking of others besides myself, I notice things I never knew before like how my elderly neighbor takes a walk by herself every day at four o'clock or how the little girl down the street plays by herself and needs a friend.

The other day I hand-painted a canvas bag. I discovered there's about a million ways I can use it to help others. For instance, I carried homemade chocolate chip cookies to bring to the new family that moved into the blue house down the street. Now I bring the bag with me everywhere I go—just in case.

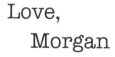

Love,
Morgan

P.S. My sister told me she thinks I'm going to be a missionary when I grow up.

Jot it down

Now, it's your turn. Write your own letter to God and tell Him about a time you saw a need and did something about it.

_____

_____

_____

_____

_____

_____

_____

_____

_____

_____

_____

_____

_____

Do not forget to do good and to share with others,
for with such sacrifices God is pleased.

Hebrews 13:16

REAL Life 101 ◀━━━━

CALLING = serving God by using your gifts.

You won't have to look very far to find ways to serve others in your community. Here are twenty-five ideas to show others you care, but before taking action, make sure you have permission from a parent.

1. Read a book to a young child.

2. Go for a walk with a senior citizen in your neighborhood.

3. Raise money for a local charity.

4. Clean up a section of the beach or park.

5. Help a neighbor plant flowers.

6. Volunteer at a local animal shelter.

7. Donate books to your library or school.

8. Write a letter to your favorite teacher.

9. Recycle.

10. Visit someone in the hospital.

11. Gather your friends and sing Christmas carols at a nursing home.

12. Collect coats for foster children.

13. Bake cookies and bring them to your local police station or firehouse.

14. Bring infant clothes and toys to a pregnancy resource center.

15. Smile often.

16. Give someone your place in line.

17. Walk a neighbor's dog.

18. Encourage others to wear bike helmets.

19. Organize a neighborhood welcome committee.

20. Make a care package for a soldier.

21. Serve a meal at a homeless shelter.

22. Be a buddy to a child with special needs.

23. Listen when others speak to you.

24. Help in the nursery at church.

25. Be a friend to a new student.

 What Does the **Bible** Say?

For even the Son of Man did not come to be served, but to serve, and to give his life as a ransom for many. Mark 10:45

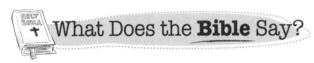 Make it!

Handprint Canvas Bag

This handy canvas bag not only looks fashionable, but also can be used to bring home groceries, hold books from the library, or carry a meal to a sick friend. As you paint this bag, think about how you can use your gifts to serve others.

What You Need:

* Canvas tote bag
* Washable fabric paint
* Paintbrush
* Fabric markers
* Newspapers

What You Do:

1. Spread newspapers on the table to protect the workspace.

2. Paint one of your hands with washable fabric paint and stamp your handprint onto the tote bag, keeping your fingers together so that it looks like a tulip.

3. Using a paintbrush and fabric paint, add leaves and a stem.

4. Write the date at the top of the bag with the markers and sign your name.

5. Let it dry.

 Write down the memory verse from the beginning of the chapter. Memorize it. List ways you can seek God's kingdom by putting others first.

_____

_____

God created you to do good works. When you find ways to help others, it brings glory to God and joy to your heart.

 Prayer **Dear God,** thank you for making me unique. Help me to serve You. In Jesus' name, Amen.

Answers

Chapter 1:

Proverbs 16:3 – Commit, establish, plans

Proverbs 19:21 – plans, heart, LORD's purpose

Proverbs 21:5 – plans, profit, haste, poverty

Jeremiah 29:11 – plans, LORD, prosper, harm, hope, future

Ephesians 5:15-16 – careful, live, unwise, opportunity, evil

Chapter 3:

Ruth
Jonathan
Ahithophel
Elisha
Pharaoh's cupbearer
Paul
Judas

Chapter 4:

"Flee the **evil** desires of youth and pursue **righteousness, faith, love** and **peace,** along with those who call on the **Lord** out of a **pure heart.**"

~ 2 Timothy 2:22

Chapter 9:

love
joy
peace
patience
kindness
goodness
faithfulness
gentleness
self-control
Fruit of the Spirit

Chapter 10:

Crossword puzzle

Across

1. Abel
4. Barnabas
5. Magi
6. Poor Widow
7. Hezekiah
9. Jesus Christ

Down

1. Abram
2. Cornelius
3. Jacob
8. Zacchaeus

Chapter 10: Match-up

Matthew 6:31-32
So do not worry, saying, 'What shall we eat?' or 'What shall we drink?' or 'What shall we wear?'

Matthew 7:11
If you, then, though you are evil, know how to give good gifts to your children,

Luke 12:7
Indeed, the very hairs of your head are all numbered.

John 21:6
He said, "Throw your net on the right side of the boat and you will find some."

Philippians 4:19
And my God will meet all your needs

Don't be afraid; you are worth more than many sparrows.

according to the riches of his glory in Christ Jesus.

how much more will your Father in heaven give good gifts to those who ask him!

For the pagans run after all these things, and your heavenly Father knows that you need them.

When they did, they were unable to haul the net in because of the large number of fish.

Chapter 11: Word Search

Horizontal and vertical answers are shaded rather than circled.

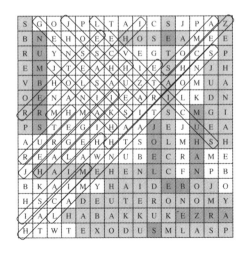